Blank Canvas

F*CK IT, I'LL PAINT!

Sicola Elliott

Published by Brush Work Motivation, Inc.
Copyright © 2019 Sicola Elliott

Editor: Lisa M. Sundry, Dragon Lady Editing
www.dragonladyediting.com

Design: LeAnna Weller Smith, Weller Smith Design
www.wellersmithdesign.com

ISBN-Hardcover: 978-0-57-857552-0
ISBN-Paperback: 978-0-57-853707-8

To order a copy of this book, please contact:
sicolaelliott@gmail.com

DEDICATION

TO MY HUSBAND
thank you for allowing me to dream.

TO JACOB, HALEY AND JADEN
all my brushstrokes in life are for you.

TO MY MOM AND DAD
thank you for your love and support, and for showing me what life is like when people are willing to do the work and change.

TO MY FAMILY
I'm sure most of you didn't even know I was writing a book! ~ but I love you all.

TO MY PEOPLE
and you know who you are ~ thank you for the realness that you bring to my life.

and...

TO OPRAH
You are a mentor to me even though you have no idea who I am. But that's the great thing about energy; it transcends. I continue to be inspired by the way you move through life and what you represent.

Thank you.

Your picture will always make my vision board.

CONTENTS

INTRODUCTION

It is three o'clock on a Saturday afternoon. I am sitting in my office listening to motivational speeches on YouTube, surrounded by stacks (and stacks) of Oprah magazines that I am looking through and cutting up for a collage I am creating.

I can hear the television from the den. It sounds as if we have surround sound wired throughout the house. We don't; my nine-year-old just acts like he is hard of hearing.

The dryer is going, and I am aware of it because I forgot to take that damn baseball belt out of my son's uniform pants, so it keeps hitting the inside liner of the dryer. I *could* get up and take it out, but my hopes are that it will just get tangled up in a shirt, which will then provide some padding, and no longer be so loud. Lazy, I know.

My eleven-year-old is immersed in his Xbox and I am sure he thinks that he's "just talking to" his friends, but he is actually *yelling* because he cannot hear himself when he has earphones on.

My husband is also here, adding his "tune" to the mix when he decides to have an outburst while watching sports. Whether his team is winning or losing—he is loud. I like to call his little outbursts "sport emotions" because no matter which side of the emotion he is on, he is really feeling it!

My daughter is quiet...which means she is either painting her nails or somewhere making a mess...along with a shitload of slime.

It sounds like I have a speaker right over my desk playing my life's soundtrack on full blast. Oh yeah, besides working on my aforementioned "Oprahllage," I'm *officially* in the middle of washing and picking up around the house—and babysitting my little niece. She's asleep currently, but should be waking up any minute in need of my attention. I have no idea what I am cooking for dinner and on top of that I still need to go to the store. But even with all this going on, I decided that today was the day I would start writing this book. What better time could there be, right?

If this were a different day, I would have gone about this task differently. I would have cleared my desk and perhaps my mind.

AHHH...YES.

I would have put on some music and made sure that everything I had to do was at least done before attempting to start. But as you and I both know: that day is never going to come. So here I am in the middle of all of this, ready to write about my blank canvas (my life) and *why I decide every day to say*, "FUCK IT, JUST PAINT."

I personally love to paint because I like how I start out with nothing and, with time, create something...and that something can be as small as one mark on a canvas. For me, painting is not entirely about the outcome, or the masterpiece that others may expect to see, if I just so happen to call myself an "artist."

It's best if we just take skill out of the whole equation.

For me, painting is all about the courage it takes to begin.

What people see or don't see within my canvas (my life) is none of my business. The only business I need to be concerned with is what I see in myself and how I feel about what I created. What we see in ourselves is the million-dollar question; but lucky for us life will provide more than a million ways for us to answer those questions. It requires courage to put paint onto a paintbrush and even more courage to transfer that paint onto a canvas. Life is all about creation and who's to say that the lines need to be perfect? Or that the thing you are attempting to paint needs to actually take shape right away? ...The Paint Gods?

In life, *we* don't take shape right away, but people often judge before things do take form, and I guess that is just something that comes with living life. But we can't be held back (OR up) by others' opinions based off of the one lens they choose to look through. Worrying about what others think keeps us from growing in so many ways. In contrast, not giving a fuck what others think is so rewarding. But like anything else, it's a skill that needs to be developed.

With people comes their opinions, thoughts, and feelings. Most of the time their advice is fueled by personal trauma and fear and, in their ignorance, they project their conditioned responses onto others. "Fuck It, Just Paint" means you go after what you want. It means you do what you have to do, learn what you have to learn in order to move yourself forward. It means that you put yourself out there even if you lack knowledge, or are scared, or even if people think you shouldn't or can't do something.

*Painting means that you start even
if the obstacles are visible and you have
to go at it alone. And you do all of this not
giving a fuck what people think.*

There are many areas in my life where I do a whole bunch of boss shit. But there have also been times where I've found myself in the back of the room, hiding. And as I stand in my truth, I am admittedly guilty of giving my *opinion, advice, two cents* from time to time; and yes, that *opinion, advice, two cents* is solely based off of my point of view, experiences, and fears.

There have been times that I have had something to say about someone else's journey, someone else's blank canvas and, more often than not, I didn't consider the other person's perspective. But—and there is a "but"—in seeking change and growth, I am at a point in my life where I simply don't have room for all the extra stuff. I think this shift came about when I turned thirty. I guess "thirty" just seemed like a big number to me and I figured by thirty I should be dishing out wisdom and not a bunch of bullshit. I took on the "I'm over here 'doing me'" attitude.

*And I want everyone to do what they
please with their blank canvas (life)...as long as
they're not trying to splash paint on mine.*

Consequently, I refrain from constantly giving my *opinion, advice, two cents* with the hope that people will notice, and in turn, treat me with the same consideration. When you begin to consciously change, you'll need to surround yourself with people who can aid and support your evolution. And although you won't give everyone permission to give you their *opinion, advice, two cents*, you will want and need people who can and will tell you the truth. You will want people to see you for who you are, and support your journey of becoming who you want to be.

The circle of people to whom I grant permission to give me feedback is really small, and even with them, I still pick and choose what I take from their thoughts and opinions. I am often challenged by my people. And I must admit that it's not easy being challenged—I mean, *I am over thirty now, right?*—but I go through it, I hear them out, and even in the moment when what they are saying may ring true, I *still* hang up the phone, stare at it and say to no one, out loud, "They don't know shit."

You have to be aware of who is in your corner and has made it onto your list of "people" because opinions carry weight; and how much you are willing to carry around can only be determined by you. You have to always remember that this is your canvas and you are the only one who has to be one hundred percent comfortable with the path that you choose.

I hate to mention this here because I feel like I am on a roll, but I should be studying for a final for a math class that I should have taken when I got out of high school. What adult besides an accountant, banker, mortgage lender, chemistry teacher, or math teacher cares about math? I have gotten along just fine adding and subtracting in my adult life.

But nevertheless, here I am. A wife. A mother of three. Today, a baby-sitter. A college student studying. A woman who needs to go to the store and prepare for the week. An artist in the middle of creating a collage. The alpha female, a.k.a. "woman of the house," doing laundry and cleaning.

But most of all, I am a woman
with a dream and a story to tell.
So today—in the midst of it all—was the perfect
day to bring a title to life.

The blank canvas represents my life and your blank canvas will represent yours. Painting births awareness, summons courage and fuels curiosity. What we get each day is the privilege of **choice**. We get to wake up each morning and choose what our lives will be.

Life is always asking us to make a choice. To
paint or not to paint.

ARE YOU READY?

Where I go with this book and my story at this point is uncharted. This book was started in the cracks of my life, in the middle of a Sunday afternoon. I am not sure where these pages will take me as I open myself up. As you read this book and journey with me through my story, I hope that you find the strength to stand up in your own story.

Life is full of riddles and I can only hope that you develop the courage to figure them out.

Don't be so hard on yourself about your failures or who failed you. And don't be anxious about moments you've never experienced—time spent worrying about shit that hasn't happened is a waste.

Never forget that looking on the brighter side is a choice, and experiencing the same obstacle until you get the lesson is a part of life.

Most importantly, make a commitment to yourself to never give up and to never stop trying to find a way to navigate through life. But if you just want to sum all of that up, just say to yourself, "Fuck it, I'll paint!"

My gift to you right now is an unlimited amount of paint so you can do just that.

CHAPTER 1

UNTANGLE

I magine this: I'm holding two gallons of paint in one hand and in the other hand I have a bunch of tangled cords. I want to paint, and I have the desire to paint, but my hands are full.

Dilemma, right?

Not really. I just have to put the paint down so I can free up that hand, because I'm going to need both hands to untangle the knots of life. Life was prompting me to do something. The easy route would have been to drop the tangled cords right where I stood, but there is no growth in that, and at that time in my life, I wanted things to start making sense.

The paint in this scenario represents courage—a supply

of courage by the gallons—so I didn't want to store it on a shelf somewhere. I needed to keep it close, because, considering the title of this book, I was going to need it. **The tangled cords** are a metaphor for all of the twists and turns in my life up to that particular moment in time. Tangled cords can be tricky because, in an effort to loosen a single knot, all that ends up happening is the others tighten even more.

So just when I think that I'm finally close to pulling the cords apart, I end up tightening the knots even more and have to start all over. I couldn't figure out how those knots got so tangled in the first place.

Same with life: you look up and all hell breaks loose. You were simply living life, and just happened to have thrown the cords all together in the same drawer. And then surprise, surprise—you end up revisiting those cords—only to reveal a giant, tangled mess. We hide and cover our "stuff" up, and then we have to decide whether to deal with our stuff or to *not* deal with our stuff.

My "stuff" was looking like an old teddy bear busting at the seams. I kept finding these tiny holes in my life where stuffing was coming out. Little by little, sprinkles of emotions would come over me.

So, I did what any normal, mature adult would do.

*I pushed that shit right back in and
kept it moving, or in this case, threw life's
cords back in a drawer.*

I mean come on, who has time to deal with all *that*? I had too much going on in my life, and I did not have the time to think about "how Little Sicola felt when she was nine." And I really didn't want to be thinking about all the things that have hurt me in my past.

When things started to come back up, I was like, "Oh, no." Not allowing feelings to fully surface seemed like the right plan of action considering the fact that I didn't want to cause myself any pain. But, to my surprise, when I pushed my stuff back into one hole, another hole would always appear. One more hole, one more cord—and one more knot. It's all the same.

My poor little bear. I just kept poking at it, hoping to keep all the stuffing in, and it looked miserable! My life was taking a turn, and the stitches were no longer holding up—not even the stitches I had sewed back up myself.

*There was a point in my life where
all the re-stuffing and re-stitching started
to become a never-ending task.*

It turns out I was actually hurting myself by trying to master the art of holding everything inside or throwing everything into the "Handle Later" drawer. It's funny how we go to school and learn so many things that we will never use; things that we will never think about again in our lives, and yet they treat this educational system like it's golden.

I would have appreciated a lesson or two on how to cope *when things change*; lessons about self-awareness, self-management, and relationship skills; or simply how to express what I am feeling in a complete sentence. These kinds of things aren't taught in school, so we grow up stuffing the shit out of our little bears.

We allow so much time to pass avoiding the tangled bits in our lives. Our happiness is tangled with our hurt; our joy is tangled with our pain; and the actions that hinder our growth are tangled with our strengths.

I don't know about you, but the only thing I want tangled with my strength is a dream. I sure as hell do not want memories of pain cuddling up with my joy. Desiring an untangled life and actually attaining a tangle-free life are two very different things. I had to ask myself, *Do I have enough courage to allow my teddy bear to explode*? My answer was, "YES!" and it continues to be yes.

Without the willingness to journey through my own story and pain, there was no way that I could help someone else journey through theirs. I knew in order to become more, I had to summon the courage to open myself up so that I could learn more. Learning more meant that I would have to face some raw reality. All the cords in my possession carried meaning and I had to discover and uncover what the story plot was and determine what role I played in each scene of my life. This is when my journey started.

My curiosity was raging, so I had to find out what I was going to do with all the cords. I had to figure out a way to get them loose from one another. I had to learn and practice patience with myself because, out of frustration...the knots would only get tighter.

My emotional bucket was on low due to lack of understanding. I had four lousy words—happy, mad, sad, or angry—to express the array of feelings that I experienced.

In order to expand upon those limited expressions, I had to educate myself and be willing to sit through a replay of my life. So here I am with a handful of cords, ready to dig in, and seeing messages everywhere that simply read, "Just be you." And I'm thinking to myself, *Easy to say, but the real question is,* "Who am I?"

Who am I? What do I like? What moves me? What sets me off? What do I need, and what does it feel like when I get it? These types of questions are what you call soul work. You can't untangle anything if you're not willing to answer some questions. It blew my mind that I did not have quick and definite answers for these questions. *There is no one else out here who can speak for me, so why is it that I cannot speak for myself?*

This was a major problem for me, if I was desiring to change other people's lives. Hell, how could I, if I didn't even know what I liked? Not knowing fully who I was was a hard pill to swallow, but I knew that in order to make a change, I had to first acknowledge what required changing. Meaning...

I had to give these cords names and call them out. My cords represented every insecurity I had, every fear I felt, every hurt I didn't want to talk about, and everything I didn't understand about life.

The one thing that was working in my favor was that I knew what I wanted to *become*. And I knew that I wanted to change the lives of young women.

My desire was to emulate the person I needed the most when I was coming of age. My goal was not to simply relate to young women, but live genuinely in my purpose so that I might be a role model to them; a guide, if you will. It became clear that I needed to pursue the journey of becoming a solid woman of integrity. Although I did not have all the answers to my questions, my curiosity started to run wild. One thing that was brought to my attention was my "why"—*why* I knew what I wanted to become before I could fully explain in plain English *who I was.*

I come from a large family consisting mainly of women. I guess you could think of us as a bunch of tangled cords, because we spent most of our summers together.

I grew up on the Westside of Long Beach and boy did we run all over that city. We laughed, fought, played, cried, sang, and said the word "anyways" with our eyes and necks rolling at least a million times a day. You name it we did it. As we grew older we all pursued different paths, and the hardest thing for me was to see someone I love go down a different path.

It left me confused. One day we were throwing barbie dolls at each other and the next everyone was dealing with life and holding their own set of tangled cords.

Not only did I want to understand it, I wanted to help. At the age of fourteen it made me wonder how things like this happen, and what the driving force was in their lives that led them down a different path. I won't say right or wrong path because we will all journey through something. I'll just say different path. Because right or wrong, our paths will be different. And how we go about untangling our lives' cords will look different as well.

My curiosity planted two questions in my heart and mind: In what ways could I help girls? And, who do I need to be in order to do so? These questions laid dormant in me for years. But just like magic, they surfaced right in the middle of me looking at my OWN handful of tangled cords.

I'm thankful for the questions that prompted this discovery.

They allowed me to make this journey—one untangled cord at a time.

CHAPTER 2

BE YOU

Be You. Two simple words that make such a strong and forceful request. This message is just about everywhere. "Live your best and authentic life." People say you have to "be you," because "everyone else is already taken." As easy as this may sound, I came to a crossroad where I lacked knowledge on the subject of "me." I truly thought that I'd be killing it in *this* area of my life by the time I reached adulthood. Nope.

More often than not, we tend to look like we have it together, when on the inside we are dry and brittle. We look the part but would crumble if someone squeezed us.

There were many areas in my life that I didn't want to touch because I was holding onto the belief that I was protecting myself from something.

You know, "protect your heart so no one can ever hurt you again"? As the brilliant Brenè Brown explains in her book, **Dare to Lead**, "We cannot selectively numb emotion. If we numb the dark, we numb the light."[1] I was building brick walls too high for anyone to climb, while needing to be loved. I needed to know more about myself, but was fearful to jump all in. But those damn "Be You" messages were everywhere.

People treat this slogan as if it's a recipe to a better life. But if being myself was supposed to be easy, why was I facing such difficulty in my attempts? If being myself was supposed to be innate, why did I feel as though I was ignorant of the true meaning of this concept?

As if it were...alien?

This is when I began experimenting with the concept of a blank canvas being a representation of my life. I began practicing "**unbecoming**" and *untangling* in order to find myself, so that I could begin to live my life genuinely. Here is a little snippet of my journey:

I went through childhood and then, just-like-that, I graduated from high school in June of 1999. (I hope that you can appreciate how I just saved you ten pages of reading about my childhood.)

---

[1]Brown, Brenè. "Dare to Lead: Brave Work. Tough Conversations. Whole Hearts." Penguin/Random House. p. 85.

I grew up loving kids, so I attended Long Beach City College to become a preschool teacher. I was a preschool teacher for a short time before I realized that I was no longer willing to earn pennies for a job that I did well. I did not know much about running a business. But at twenty, who does? All I knew was that I felt comfortable doing things my way. (Right in the middle of all of my dream-chasing, my heart was broken in October of 2000. Moving right along. I'll get back to *that.*) On April 3, 2001, I opened my own family childcare center from a place within myself that was carefree.

Because I had nothing, I had nothing to lose.

Although I was just an over-sized teenager stepping into the real world, I held high standards for myself. My parents allowed their ambitious daughter to transform their living room into a space that would service the needs and hearts of children. With their support I was able to make a move on what I desired. I got married in 2004 and gave birth to my first child later that year. When he was five months old, I found out that we were expecting *another* child. She just happened to arrive a day before her brother's first birthday.

In 2007, I was blessed with another baby boy, my third and final child. At the time, I was still running a very successful business, but now out of my own home. Business was booming as usual, and I spent countless hours perfecting my craft and creating environments that would nurture the souls of the little people that walked through my door each morning.

I was in my twenties, and life from the lens I was looking through was good.

I had the flexibility to dream and the opportunity to do what I loved. I was flowing in my purpose and life accommodated me! It's funny how life works. I was just living day by day and never took a moment to ponder on the forces that existed in my surroundings. Hell, at the time, I had no clue how energetic vibrations and *flow* could affect my life.

Energy and flow are real, and I believe that if you are flowing in your purpose, life will provide.

My business continued to thrive and there was a constant stream of newly enrolled children. Life yielded many blessings. I like to think that I received back every ounce of energy that I put into working towards my dreams, and then some, because I had the courage to try.

During the seventh year of running my successful business, my passion began to take me in a different direction. Something else was burning on the inside of me. I still loved my business, I still loved and adored the children I cared for, but thoughts and ideas that were planted on the inside of me—without notice—left the stage of curiosity and started to bud.

In 2008, I decided to turn my collection of middle school and high school poetry into a book entitled, **Pocket Book of Poems from a Teenage Heart**, and I still had the feeling that there was more I needed to become. There were things about me that I wanted to uncover. I can even say it felt like something was *missing*. I was content...but not fully fulfilled. Something I just couldn't put my finger on or attach words to inside of me was shifting.

My cords were untangling:

"How do I choose between the minds of children and the hearts of teenagers?"

When I think about it now, they are damn near the same thing. When I'm working with a teenage girl who's having a fit, all I see is a five-year old in front of me. But back then, it felt as if I were choosing between two totally different professions. This is when all the questions started to come up. The easy part was knowing what I wanted to become—Oprah. Okay, my OWN (no pun intended) version of Oprah. The hard part was knowing exactly how to get there.

*I had to ask life to reveal to me
what I didn't know or what I needed to
understand about myself in order to more
fully **BECOME ME.***

CHAPTER 3

THE SCARY PART

Change on any level is scary. And it scared me a whole lot that I was considering closing the doors of my childcare business to embark on a new adventure. Even though I was receptive to the desire guiding me to my next journey, I often found myself debating on whether ending my business was the correct decision. If I did not love my childcare anymore, what did I love? If my childcare no longer defined me, what would? I was afraid of losing what I considered to be my life's passion, for it was how I had defined myself for so long. I felt stuck because I was so confused and afraid.

I questioned whether the signs were real or if I was just tripping.

I was in a tug of war—with myself. On the one hand, I fought to keep my passion alive for my childcare business, while on the other hand I kept fighting to choose myself over everything. I was simultaneously fighting to gain my own identity, while attempting to preserve the only avenue that I felt defined me for so long. I had opened my childcare two months after I turned twenty. I never devoted much time to nurturing or exploring my identity outside of being a childcare provider. One day I was a teenager just out of school, and the next I was a business owner with more responsibilities than I could have ever imagined. The struggle was real, because I had always dreamed about the childcare facility I would one day open. And now, to just leave that behind me?

Feeling the pull hurt me in many ways. Giving up on what I thought my life would be was hard to do. I was being stretched and was overwhelmed with all kinds of emotions.

Not surprisingly, I was fatigued for many reasons. Being a business owner comes with many perks, but it also comes with many issues and things to work through. You have to have a strong mind in order to put things in perspective and carry on. If there was one thing that I could do, it was to motivate myself to keep going no matter what. But I got to a point where I no longer possessed the energy or drive to do so.

I knew then that it was time to make a move, but I was sitting on the fence; well, more like clinging to the fence.

On June 18, 2012, my journal entry reads:

> *I want to stop the childcare business because I feel trapped. But even feeling trapped, I don't want to let anyone down. I am a fighter, but sixty-five percent of me doesn't even want to win the fight. I want to change, but I'm scared. I want to say no, but most of the time I end up saying yes.* I feel like giving up.

I was surprised that giving up was even an option I entertained. I guess you can say I felt a little helpless. I wanted to choose myself, I just had a hard time doing so. My daily affirmation, *"Don't let fear get in the way of you pulling the plug,"* helped me put one foot in front of the other and make a move.

I pondered this for an entire year and, in June of 2013, I took a deep breath, swallowed the lump in my throat and wrote a memo to my clients to inform them that, as of August 3rd, 2013, the doors of Sicola's Family Childcare would close for good. The time had come. I would no longer allow fear to hinder my forward movement. I had a bucket full of "what if" questions, but all I could do at the time was acknowledge their presence and continue to move.

Closing my childcare broke my heart.

However, life after The Big Close
started changing fast.

The room full of bright colors, the lingering sound of children laughing, and the smell of oatmeal and toast in the morning was quickly fading. It would now become just another room in my house. I knew the moment that I applied the first coat of white primer paint to the walls that life as I knew it would never be the same.

I could feel my own resistance with every
stroke of the paint roller.

I just painted and cried.

But as I prepped the walls for the new décor, I was also prepping for a new life. In order to follow through with uncovering my true destiny, I knew that I had to muster the courage to finally choose myself. As I stood in the middle of that hollow room painting primer over a piece of my life, two questions ran through my mind:

What do I do now? And for real this time—"Who am I?"

Talk about a blank canvas...

CHAPTER 4

THE MORNING AFTER

There will always be a "morning after" any decision we make. The funny thing about that is when I think of a "morning after," for some strange reason I think of a one-night stand. You might be saying to yourself, "Well, that's not strange, Sicola; that's what 'the morning after' usually is referring to." Okay, but you see, I have never had a one-night stand, so I do not have firsthand experience of the emotions felt "the morning after." I have, however, watched enough TV and have quite the imagination!

Needless to say, I get the gist. The following is a fictional anecdote of how I imagine the morning after a one-night stand would take place for me:

I would wake up not knowing where the hell I am and

would have no recollection of what happened the night before. My thoughts would be racing. I would attempt to swiftly recollect the previous night's events, as I hear the rapid approach of footsteps. I'm sure I would then go into full-blown panic mode trying to wake my memory up, demanding answers from it—at least some visuals, a name, *something*—before the footsteps turn into a full-grown human body standing in front of me. Don't get me wrong; I'm sure this human body would represent all the finer things in life. "Eye candy" times ten! But those feelings of attraction would be obsolete once I checked back in to the reality of being unfamiliar with his body. I imagine that I would not be familiar with his six pack, his muscular arms, and the other essential details—which I will just say would of course be a gift from God himself.

(Can I get an "Amen!"?)

After initially seeing him enter the room in all of his glory and getting past all of that, most likely I would scream. And that screaming would then turn into me throwing up.

Now, that upheaval would not be from me having too much to drink. Anyone who knows me, knows that I do not like liquor, and therefore do not drink. I would be throwing up because in order for me to be naked in an unknown place, with an unknown person, I would have had to have been drugged. I'm such a drama queen, so I'm sure it would have been quite a scene.

I would be sick to my stomach, lost, confused, and contemplating the decisions I had made in the midst of my stupor that would have brought me to this moment in my life.

The morning after closing my childcare made me feel something like this. I know it sounds a bit dramatic, but I woke up with the same sentiments expressed in my hypothetical morning-after predicament; however, there was no one to blame for me being "drugged" besides myself. Yes, in my fictional "morning after," I did wake up to someone that I did not know.

Conversely, in real life, I ended up being the stranger in the room with me. I not only felt naked, but also invisible. I felt that I had done something *wrong* because nothing was clear.

It felt like my soul had faded away. I was lost. I had an *emotional hangover* because I was pretty fucked up the night before. And now, in the light of day, my drug (i.e. hysteria) was gone. I had ended what I perceived to be the thing that filled the voids of my life, if any; and now that thing was gone. The echo of that emptiness reverberated within.

"FUCK! What the hell did I just do?!"

I cut off my income with zero means of alternate compensation—*who does that*? And now I was in front of the mirror looking back at a reflection that I failed to recognize.

My "morning after" made me feel small. I felt like something was taken from me. And questions just filled my mind. Did I mess up? Is this other passion something I made up in my head? Was I actually having a great time with my childcare and then closed it just because of a few bad days? Did I just throw away all that I had worked so hard for? Was this the right choice? My "morning-after" had my mind spinning. I felt guilty because I thought I had let people down.

My symptoms were akin to a night filled with poor decision making, fueled by unwillingly ingesting drugs. I woke up in a poor mental state, my emotions were all over the place, and I felt like shit. There were so many questions running through my mind, and at the time the answers were nowhere to be found.

I felt like I was watching a really twisted movie, and I wanted to save the girl from the cringe-worthy scene.

I wanted to yell, "Get up and get out!"

But I could not, because all of my energy was gone.

Additionally, I resonated a little too much with that girl; and everyone knows that it is easier to save strangers than it is to help yourself. Apparently I had not only built my life around my childcare business, but also my self-identity. In the world of child-care, there are so many factors that the business and lifestyle encompass. I had been attached to observing the children's development in the childcare space, and I had also been invested in their families and their life experiences out in the world. When you think about it, there really was no "me" identity in that equation.

Although my decision ultimately empowered me, I was initially incapable of fully recognizing and owning that power. The ambivalence of my feelings—the positive emotions mixed with negative emotions—drove me insane. I had poured everything into my childcare; even the last, tiny bit of energy that remained at the end of a long day.

Like most relationships, you never want to be the one to call it off. It's not like I wanted the Department of Social Services to come in and shut me down, but when you don't have enough courage to put yourself before all else, self-sabotage presents itself as the best and easiest option. It takes courage to say, enough is enough. For me, that did not come easy. I absolutely do not like to rock the boat. Amidst all of the "morning after" feelings, I had the nerve to top it off with fear.

Just as an artist feels overwhelmed with insecurity and doubt—unsure of where or how to make the first mark on a blank canvas—I was also reeling with uncertainty in regard to dealing with the aftermath of emotions following this huge, life-altering decision.

I had no idea where this path would lead and wasn't clear on how I felt, but I did know that there was work to be done, so I made self-reflection my Number One priority—and therein held the brushes in hand with which to paint on this new blank canvas.

CHAPTER 5

LITTLE SICOLA

After closing the doors to my childcare business, my best friend and I discovered an author by the name of Brenè Brown. Perhaps you noticed that I quoted Brenè Brown in an earlier chapter; however, I didn't mention that my friend and I thought we "discovered" her before Oprah did. I'll wait, because I know you are laughing, but it's true. To this very day, we remain humored by our foolishness. Brenè Brown is a researcher who studies vulnerability, courage, and shame. I dived head first into three of her books: *The Gifts of Imperfection, I Thought It Was Just Me,* and *Daring Greatly.* Each of these works resonated heavily with me; page after page, I madly highlighted and underlined every ounce of inspiration that jumped from the print to the pit of my stomach.

Cumulatively, the varying marks and fluorescent blocks dancing around specific words, statements, and ideas, created an almost coloring-book effect throughout my copies of her tomes. Her books caused me to contemplate and consequently explore the depths of my soul. Her book, *The Gifts of Imperfection: Let Go of Who You Think You're Supposed to Be and Embrace Who You Are*, pretty much sums up my journey. I *was* letting go of what I thought I would be and who I thought I would be while embracing who I actually was even though that was not very clear yet.

Newly unemployed, I was able to get a glimpse of what the silence of life felt like.

Running a childcare business and being a mother, there weren't many moments of pure silence that I can recall. But not having a *J-O-B* made this silence more accessible. I guess that was life's way of giving me the okay to finally allow Little Sicola to roar and let her existence be known.

After I wrote the title to this chapter, I just stared at the page. Nothing came to mind instantly. As a matter of fact, in that moment it was as if I had to give my childhood a moment of silence, followed by a deep inhale and then exhale.

After that moment, I was reminded of a picture of myself when I was around six years old. My grandparents lived on a busy street on the Westside of Long Beach, California and they had a faded blue bus stop right in front of their house. Cars were constantly in motion, but in this picture not one car was in sight. It was just me sitting alone at the bus stop. My face was dressed with a half-smile. My hair was in a few pigtails. And I was sitting on my feet, with my back facing the street, and one hand tightly gripping the bus stop post. I had on a turtleneck and some shorts, so I'm guessing I dressed myself that day. Although I did not look scared, the awkward positioning of my hand gripping the bus stop post let me know that my instincts were in gear. I know that I wasn't alone and was probably told a million times to get off of the bus stop and away from the street. But there I was.

Reflecting on the picture made me wonder what I was thinking. What was my family going through at the time? How I was feeling? Or, was I just sitting there because that's what we did when we needed to take a break from running wild? I highly doubt that I had nothing on my mind because I was always thinking about something, but the picture captured a rare moment of stillness.

As a child, my maternal and paternal grandparents lived around the corner from each other. To put it in perspective, they lived five houses apart. My siblings, cousins, and I spent summers running back and forth between their respective houses. If we got kicked out of one house for being too boisterous or disobedient, which

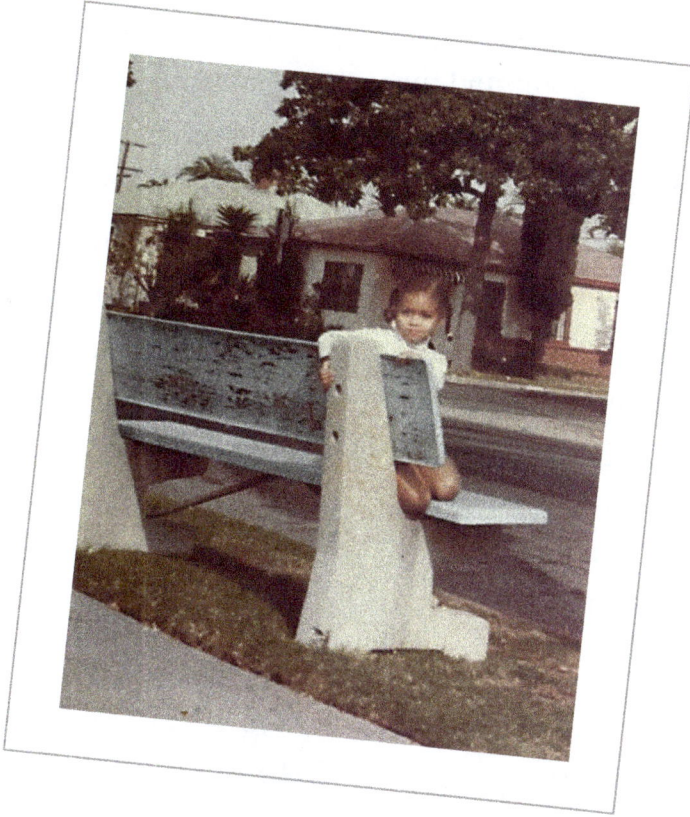

happened often, we would just go around the corner to our other grandparents' house. Two different households, two different sets of rules.

We ran wild and it drove my grandparents crazy.

My maternal grandmother would let us do just about anything. We were always trying to find ways to make money so we could run to the store fifty thousand times. I remember we made applesauce once, put it in used baby food jars, and went door to door selling our homemade applesauce for one shiny dime each.

My paternal grandparents were different; more serious, and we weren't allowed to run in and out. If we were out, we were out. There was no coming back and forth. We hated it, so we used to pretend that we had to use the restroom to get back into the house in order to walk through the kitchen and grab a handful of the lemon cookies my grandmother always kept on hand. I loved my grandparents, and it was nice being able to see them each day.

Having so many cousins, we were always up to something and into everything.

Going back and forth to the corner liquor store, which we called "The Dairy," was one of our favorite pastimes. The owner's name was Robert, and he both loved and hated us. If we came to the store more than once in a single day with a hand full of pennies, he would kick us out. Sometimes we would get sassy and give him a hard time, but really, there was no need. There were so many of us that we would just take turns going into the store.

LITTLE SICOLA

I remember being able to buy packs of cigarettes as a minor, simply equipped with a handwritten note from my grandmother. I guess the world had more trust in the youth back then.

Regardless, I knew that I had zero interest in smoking those cigarettes myself. The deal was, if you were the kid to get the cigarettes for the day, you were set, because the spare change from sales was plenty, and you'd then be able to purchase a day's supply of Now and Laters. Now and Laters were and still are my favorite candy. (I often shock the store attendant to this day when my grown self walks into a liquor store and asks them to hand me eight packs of watermelon-flavored Now and Laters. Don't judge me. The kid in me still wants to live.)

My siblings, cousins, and I played all over the Westside. We had no pagers and no cell phones. We just...*played.* The streetlights kept track of time for us, and we had each other to keep busy and stay entertained.

Little Sicola is a huge topic for me. I thought my newfound occupation of self-discovery would be like an internship, where I would ease my way into the heavy lifting of the task; you know, take my time to gain experience that would enable me to work through some of the things I felt as a child. But herein lies one of the most startling tasks of my personal development:

In order to discover myself I had to be open to whatever came up once I started digging for answers.

I also had to be willing to deal with what was at hand at the time. I knew I would get to Little Sicola during the discovery process; I just didn't think it would be right out the gate. I was thinking that she would be buried under other life issues and not so close to the surface, but there she was. Though as a child Little Sicola seemingly lacked much to say aloud, it did not mean that she didn't desire to be heard.

My childhood is full of good memories. Full of things that make me smile and laugh for hours. There were more good times than bad, but the bad times were plenty—and the understanding I needed was lost somewhere in between those two realities.

I grew up in dysfunction. I didn't find out until later in life that, in some way, shape, or form, dysfunction is everywhere and can be found in just about any family.

Dysfunction has many different faces and shows up in our lives in many different ways. Some ways are extreme and others are not, but at the core of things, it's all the same. It's the feeling that something is *just not right*. It's funny that when you are a kid

44

you think that it's only your crazy family and you go through life thinking others have it better or handle life better.

The dysfunction that I experienced was domestic violence. I grew up in it, and it seemed like my world was perpetually falling apart. I constantly worried about things going from good to bad in the blink of an eye and there were many times I felt unsafe and on edge.

Little Sicola did not learn about dysfunction in school; she lived it. I was a quiet kid with a lot going on in my head. My mom and aunties love to tell stories about how I would silently hold up two fingers in response to their comments towards me. Though they laugh when recounting these stories, I do not find my response, in any way, humorous. Maybe my behavior was indicative of a need, but as I look back, maybe it was the budding of my rebellious spirit. That rebellious spirt can be "something else" to deal with, but it has actually helped me in life—in the times I've put the right energy behind it.

Growing up in a world that was plagued with domestic violence, a lot of my childhood was cloaked in a veil of uneasiness and insecurity. I lived in a world where I completely lacked control when it came to my foundation—my constantly-at-war parents. Even though my mom did a great job making sure that we had what we needed, I always suspected, and experientially knew, that the "good times" would not last; and, without fail, would soon meet their true destiny.

Sometimes it felt as if good times did not exist and were simply bad times that had yet to come to fruition.

As a child you are helpless, because there is really nothing that you can do about the circumstances, especially with something you don't fully understand. You're crippled by helplessness while living in the space of pure innocence. I was a child faced with the realities of adulthood and all the issues, perspectives, and decisions that come with it. I was convinced that others had betters lives and often wondered how I landed a spot in my family. Not being privy to the information that most people grow up in some kind of dysfunction, I spent my childhood dreaming that someone would rescue me when times were really bad, and sometimes it was all I could think about.

Hell, I wanted someone to rescue my mom. I don't know how she did it. She had the ability to expose us to her strength even when she was in pain. My parents fought all the time, and the fighting adapted, transformed, and evolved into a typical occurrence of what I considered to be a mundane aspect of life.

Just as a child comes to understand the recurrence and necessity of dinner and a bath, I budded in a household where dysfunction was not only the norm, but expected. I was an 80's baby, and a lot of families including mine were affected by the crack epidemic. My dad started using drugs, and my mom used alcohol as a coping mechanism. Their vices combined threw my life into utter chaos and hell.

The day after any fight, we were still expected to get up and get ready for school. The smell of liquor would be in the air, and potting soil and broken glass littered our sight.

Post-fighting mornings, my dad was either gone or in jail. Oh yeah, the police were all too familiar with our address. My grandfather would be the one to pick us up in the morning and drop us off to the bus. Sending us off to learn our math facts and bring our grades up. I would wonder, "How?" My mind was plagued with the disturbing images that I was forced to endure the night before, not to mention I was in class thinking that this kind of stuff only happened in my house and with my family.

My home environment shaped me into a confused and insecure girl, and at a very young age I came to my own conclusions. Little Sicola's only focus was protecting her heart. In the process of protecting myself from hurt, I began to reject my mother, honing in on the fear that I would develop into her.

I feared inheriting my mother's life—her pain, even her endurance. Although she displayed great strength and I admired that strength, I

resented her for her weaknesses that I couldn't understand.

She did what she had to do while feeling pain and disappointment, but I still wanted nothing to do with those traits. Despite these adult feelings, fears, and apprehensions, I still recall my childhood with fondness. I mean, come on—the best part about being a kid is being a kid! Considering the recurring drama and tension that I endured in my home life, I still had fun. My childhood cannot be entirely reduced to bad memories. There was love, and there was laughter. My parents loved my siblings and me the best way that they possibly could at the time. It was what they knew, and they did their absolute best. That is knowledge that can only be achieved through age and maturity, because I definitely did not have that perspective as a child.

There were a variety of things that allowed me to have a typical childhood. I lived in a realm where I could take part in imaginative play. I had loving grandparents and an entire army of cousins that lightened my "family life" experience. And on most days, that was all I needed.

Life is crazy; and on top of that we do not have the luxury of choosing the family that we are born into. Even if we did, I know now that they would still come with their own set of problems. Having the opportunity to be born into a species and body of consciousness is a gift and I'm grateful that someone had me.

I have learned that it must never be forgotten that our parents are people.

Parents are flawed people, learning and trying their best, just like you and me. The only difference is that, on one particular day, your parents conceived and (later) gave birth to you. I am the fourth of six children; the youngest being my half-brother. My maternal grandmother suffered from mental illness. Back in the day, an atypical emotional expression was typically classified as a "nervous breakdown." My grandmother was diagnosed with schizophrenia in her latter twenties. My paternal grandparents were driven, successful, functioning alcoholics.

In addition to love, the dynamics of our dysfunction run deep. My mom has loved my dad since they were in the third grade. She was very shy and did not talk much. She was even worse when he would come around, because she would become mute. To this day, she lights up when she tells the stories of how beautiful he was. She talks about his silky, curly hair and how he just blew her away. Let her tell it, he was dreamy and she fell hard in love. She tells the story about the day he moved into the neighborhood. She and her friend watched from across the street as everything seemed to move in slow motion when my dad walked out of that house.

The love that my mom has for my dad is rooted deep. On a certain level, I know somewhat the extent of how that attachment feels. But damn, we're talking about the third grade here.

Not every love story has a happy ending, because most people are not willing to do the work, and change when life calls us to; but my mom and dad's love story does. My parents are still together. Though their love is fruitful, there is trauma that I continue to journey through to this day, as their child. Little Sicola was full of life but lacked a sense of security, and my childhood experiences are still embossed on my heart and mind. I remained silent while my heart screamed.

And like every child, Little Sicola became a woman. Funny how that happens, right? Our bodies grow and age reflects how long we have been here, but emotionally we are stuck. While my body grew, my emotional needs had not yet been fully met. I guess that's why we get into our twenties and then blame everything on our parents, as if it's a natural, universal law.

I turned into a woman who did not fully understand all that went on in her life. The lessons on love had been mixed with pain, disappointment, and confusion.

As I got to work untangling my cords,
Little Sicola—in all her innocence—held the
tools that I needed.

I had to find a way to merge the gap between the woman I had become and Little Sicola, for the benefit of both. Little Sicola possessed the most important paint and paintbrushes that the world could ever offer. She is a gift to me, and I now understand what my immature mind couldn't:

Personal power is not given,
it's discovered.

CHAPTER 6

SHOVEL IN THE GROUND

It was not long before I realized that ending my childcare business also meant that the daily demands an entrepreneur, such as myself, becomes accustomed to also come to an end. Emotional digging became my full-time profession. It's not a job I would have applied for, but nevertheless, there I was.

Being unemployed felt weird, and the new identity I was wearing felt more like an itchy sweater.

I was a bit irritated by the fact that I didn't feel right in my own skin. I had layers of worry and fear, and although excitement existed in the midst of it all, the itchy-sweater feeling lingered. It was brought to my attention that every heartbreak, regret, joy, step forward or backwards is experienced because we are meant to learn specific lessons at particular times—lessons that are calculated and ordained according to universal law and order.

Desiring to live my truth, I knew that it was imperative for me to continue to dig, explore, and be open to understanding more about myself and this life that I had incarnated into. Getting to know myself was a personal mission. I did not seek anyone's approval. Although personal growth and enhancement was a desire, it felt like more of a necessity; a birthright.

To my surprise, paintbrushes were everywhere. As was a shovel. The biggest shovel one could buy at a store, along with some random power tools.

Each tool lay idly waiting for the moment
that I would choose it, pick it up,
and activate its eager, dormant inspiration—
turning it into power.

Now that I had Little Sicola on board, it was time to get dirty and dig up what I had buried over the years. I needed to make myself see the things that I had grown blind to, and sift through it all. I needed to experience the feelings that I was initially incapable of giving a voice or a name to. I could have called someone in to do the digging for me, but I knew that I needed to hold the shovel in the palm of both of my hands and do the digging for myself.

Unfortunately, I overdid it with the size of the shovel, because it was heavy as hell and the dirt's resistance was akin to the impossible nature of concrete. It was very tough and hard to get through! But against all odds, yours truly was eager to persevere.

I put that big-ass shovel in a ready position, placed both of my feet on top of it like a pogo stick, and gave that shovel two hundred pounds of body force (give or take) and dug up nothing but...pain?

Now that's one hell of a discovery.

That discovery made this canvas seem overwhelmingly large, and instead of wanting to paint it, I just kind of wanted to set it on fire and watch it burn. Turns out, I had given my childcare business and clients everything my broken heart hadn't given me. *Broken heart?* I was shocked and amazed to be able to put that into words, although they didn't sound right coming out of my mouth. I had to stand up, dust off my clothes, and step back for a moment.

I was like, "What?! What broken heart?" because I have had a few. With no details or insight into which one or at "which time," I was a bit confused. In the moment, I knew that the missing detail didn't matter, and given the heaviness of this shovel, I knew it couldn't be just one isolated incident, either.

This was big. No, this was huge—because it was a collection of all the times I had felt pain in my life. I was thinking to myself, *So you buried it all in one place huh?* And then I moved on to a more positive note and thought to myself, *Well, at least you didn't have to spend years digging, because it's all here.*

Most people spend their twenties attempting to "find themselves." We either experience success, or lack thereof. Throughout the duration of my twenties, I had the privilege of getting to know what everyone *else* was about. I overlooked the opportunity to discover what worked for me, and that cloudiness allowed various lessons and opportunities to go unnoticed.

Even though I was standing on shaky ground, I could see how Life had always been preparing me in some way, shape, or form to walk my path.

I knew that any path would get me somewhere, I just had to determine if that "somewhere" was somewhere I wanted to be.

All paths in life are full of signs and nuggets of valuable information. Sometimes we drift off our path and are detoured to another route. And although detours are an inconvenience for everyone, valuable takeaways can be found within them. "Takeaways" meaning—*anything that is left behind or uncovered during the obstacle.*

I was learning how to work from my takeaways. And although I was standing in front of dusty memories of pain, thinking, "What could these dusty ass memories possibly want from me?" I had to take full responsibility for digging them up. *But damn, what am I to do with them now*? I wondered in awkward pain.

Life placed at my feet all of my broken pieces, and although many people don't find value in broken pieces, I had to honor and respect mine.

> **Then I got to thinking, "Maybe I should have used a rake instead. Was the timing even right for all this mess?"**

If I was being called to do something great, then by all means let things roll, but this canvas was asking me to paint and confront the things that had broken me into tiny little pieces.

Then I remembered that I had opened my childcare business while I was hurting; when I felt most alone. I had forgotten that tiny detail. My broken heart had not made me feel secure, so I had provided security for others and, consequently, myself. I nurtured my business so it could never go numb.

I had not only loved it, but I appreciated it. I had given it more of myself every day. I made sure that I was good at what I did, and when "good" wasn't good enough, I made myself better. My business was like this breathing thing that loved me back and I trusted in its abilities. It was mine, and I would not betray it or do anything to jeopardize my hard work. I loved it unconditionally. It was the spark in my imperfect world because I was able to create it. *Creating* filled the void of all the confusion I was carrying around.

Hearing myself say, "You opened your childcare with a broken heart," was life changing. Because what I was really saying is that I had built a life on top of pain.

> **I didn't intend to "open up a childcare to fill voids in my life"; that just ended up being the case.**

I knew the pain was there because it showed up from time to time. But the depths of it had been hidden underneath my creativity, children's cries, their laughter, and the busyness of life. I never had the time (and didn't make the time) to really deal with the things that had caused me pain; nor did I have the tools in my toolbox to even work through it before then.

I *should* list all the synonyms for the word "Pain" because each word represents what I was feeling while standing next to my tool of choice, that damn shovel. But in order to spare you having to read through me explaining my hurt using fifty different words which mean the same thing—I'll just leave it at that.

Okay, and this: in that moment, my heart felt as if it had been ripped from my body and stomped on. And since it was already on the ground, it sure did seem like a good time to just kick it in the hole, scoop the dirt that I had dug up and bury this once again, taking my chances at "life" holding it in.

But in order to be present with my emotions, I knew I had to be *present*. I had to willingly take myself back in time and allow myself to feel. The thought of it, the thought of feeling those old feelings, made my stomach turn and my heart ache. But that wasn't the hardest part.

> ***The hardest part was feeling something on the inside that had nothing to do with my current life—and at the same time had everything to do with it.***

Love is the magic key to unlock or lock any door, and I wanted to transform my life with it. But I also needed to understand all the bruises and pain it had caused me.

In searching for the answers, I started thinking about everything I had built in my life: a marriage, a family, a successful business, and functioning relationships with people. But marriage and having kids did not make me forget the pain I had experienced in my childhood, nor the trauma that carved its way into my path as a young adult. If by chance you happen to stumble across a partner, or friendship, or relationship that has made you forget your past traumas—keep them, because that shit is pure magic. But in real life, and in my life, there were no magic wands that I could wave to erase my past. I did, however, discover that although a partner, friendship, or relationship were not cures for my "condition"—they sure were some damn good reasons to deal with my trauma and move on.

Love comes with no guarantees and those lessons are not only difficult to learn, but can also be pretty painful as well.

There wasn't anything filling my time during this blank canvas in my life; I had very little distraction outside of being a mother and a wife, so I could no longer ignore the nagging emotions.

Growing up, we learn from what we see and are able to touch in our environment, and I learned that you love unconditionally. Well, that was the unspoken message I got, anyway. And it's not a bad lesson, depending on the context. Knowing how to love and how to establish healthy boundaries is a gift. A gift you can't fully tap into until you begin to understand all of the moving parts of love. I'm not sure if we will ever be able to pinpoint all the moving parts, but what I do know is that the lessons only come from real life experiences.

It became clear to me that I couldn't rid myself of hurt and disappointment—by using hurt and disappointment as a tool. I couldn't combat confusion with confusion, so I had to get a clear view of everything—behind me, within me, and around me. Only clarity would help me understand the existence of these remaining feelings of the past...while pushing forward dealing with the ebbs, flows, and nuances of current life.

> **I didn't understand why love came with pain. In fact, I had written this very scene out of my life when I was a child.**

This message was never clear growing up, not sure if it could have been. Probably not. I was trying to show up for myself better than I thought my mom had for herself. Trying to display the "strength" I had wished she'd had, as I understood strength. I wanted no part or ownership of this struggle in my life. To continue to love anyone who had hurt me would have felt like I was betraying my inner child.

That feeling alone carried its own weight. I was not only dealing with the pains of life, I was faced with everything Little Sicola did not understand growing up. This is not about a romantic love, although it plays a part. This was about the principle and standard Little Sicola had declared about love as a child. This was about everything that four-letter word encompasses.

Love comes packaged as a bundle. It comes with hurt, pain, joy, laughter, understanding, fulfillment, you name it. But hurt and pain will have you thinking that the other things never existed.

Growing up I didn't see how they could. One reason being that, as a kid, none of it made sense. How could the greatest power on earth, love, have an opposite effect? How could this magical, powerful thing end in grief? And it's quite simple. Just as there are casualties of war there are also casualties of life and love. Although we do not volunteer for that role, we often are handed the script.

I have learned that, in some circumstances, we are the casualty of someone else's life lessons.

I am the casualty of my parents' pain. Although that was not their aim, there was damage done. I was caught in *their* crossfire. And those painful experiences are hard to understand when the unexpected reality of our own choices—or someone else's choices—hits home.

As I sat with the dusty old pain, I realized that the hurt that comes from love, or loving someone and being hurt by them, did not mean that I had to relinquish the happy memories and joys I felt. That was indeed the biggest conflict and misconception in my life.

People who loved me deeply had hurt me for one reason or another because that's a part of life. Everyone is on a different growth wave. But if I stood now to face a question that, in my hurt, I could never answer—*Do you think they hurt you intentionally?*—my answer would be ninety-seven percent, "No." (The other three percent would be, "Hell, yes!" but that is so small it doesn't even matter.)

My desire at that moment was to break free of the things that kept me down, and since love was the feeling and action that could change my world, I had to decide that the hurt did not supersede it.

I had to be open to the fact that life is indeed painful, but that most of those pains are pushing us to grow, and every situation has something to teach us if we are willing to learn. We spend a lot of time labeling experiences in life as either "good" or "bad," but there are so many options in between those two extremes.

I WAS NOW EXPLORING THE OTHER OPTIONS.

CHAPTER 7

JUST DECIDE

When I come to a crossroad in my life I can always hear Will Smith's voice in my head. In an interview with Tavis Smiley on the Tavis Smiley Show, Will Smith said some words that play back to me every time I need to make a choice. He said, "You just decide *what* it's going to be, *who* you're going to be, and *how* you're going to do it. Just decide." He said it with such conviction, as if it were the easiest thing to do.

It made me realize that I cannot get ahead in life by playing it safe all the time.

I couldn't "camp out" and think that life would magically project itself forward with little to no effort from me.

The urge to purge. I needed to decide for myself that

it was time to say no to the things and people that I no longer wanted or needed in my life, and say yes to the things and people that were aligned with where I wanted to go. Will Smith's voice echoed inside of my head and was only growing louder: just decide.

In order to decide, we have to take inventory of who we are, right where we stand.

That is a difficult, but worthy, task. _Easy task_? Of course not; I just said that it is difficult. In fact, it is one of the hardest tasks you can give a person. I had to push myself to make a list of the positive characteristics I possessed, and to be honest, I felt as if my list was kind of short. At the time I didn't get down on myself, I just took that as an indication that there was more work that needed to be done.

"Self-inventory" could mean listing what characteristics you possess or it could be a series of questions that you need to ask yourself.

Do I _respond_ or do I _react_? When I react, what am I feeling? When I respond what am I feeling? Are there people in my life that I am always reacting to? Do I give one hundred percent? What am I afraid of? These are just a few questions that I asked myself. For me, it was the starting point to identify and address my list.

In 2014, I responded to Will Smith's words and had declared that 2014 would be the year for me. What that meant was I decided to focus on me and me only.

I had this burning desire to step outside of myself and observe my performance—the good, the bad, and oh my goodness, the ugly.

At the end of 2013, I yearned for so much more. I had touched the core of some things, and although I was afraid, I wanted to go further. My best friend and I decided that we were not going to use social media for a whole year in exchange for deep, personal insight and growth. We wanted 2014 to be all about self-discovery and we knew in order for that to take place we had to give up the impulse to spend our precious time clicking through other people's lives. Social media demanded a lot of our mental space and energy, so we decided to cut it out of our lives.

I decided that I would journal for the whole year to hold myself accountable and to have something to look back on. My goal for 2014 was to make my expression of life beautiful, both inside and out. Whether this was a solo journey or one with the support of others, I had already decided and declared that it was going to be not only worth it, but great.

Anticipating my growth was exciting because I was reinventing myself. I was gathering all the pieces of my life and ready like never before to reconfigure it anew, with threads of understanding.

Thinking back, all of the life lessons that came from the experience of being a business owner were priceless. I feel empowered when I reflect on all of the power moves I have made in my life, but there were aspects of myself that had remained dormant—not ever wanting to rock the boat. I chose silence in many situations because pleasing others was the path of least resistance. But damn that: when you decide, you go big, so 2014 was going to be about courage, boundaries, and developing my voice.

No longer a childcare owner, I found myself in a hopeful, but really weird, place in my life. I questioned the skills that I had or didn't have. To be honest, the skills that I lacked kind of scared me. My confidence was up and down. I was applying for jobs that I didn't even want. Testing and interviewing for jobs I didn't get.

I mean, come on, how in the hell did they not see my brilliance? I have an answer for that now, but back then I was just confused.

It's simple: thoughts of what you lack only produce more thoughts of what you lack. There were many situations during this adjustment period that had nothing to do with my skill set and more to do with my decisions. More to do with my motives and *whys.*

I could have allowed my mind to dwell on what I lacked, but instead I decided that what I lacked was temporary—because I was willing to learn anything. It's funny how we go through life sometimes wanting things and wanting to do things and yet will not lift our baby toe to achieve it.

*The "Fall in My Lap" prayer is dead,
because anything that falls in your lap
can fall off just as fast when you have no
idea how to maintain it.*

Decision-making did not come natural for me. I often made decisions for the wrong reasons, based on how others would feel, and kind of left myself out of the equation. I often tell that Will Smith voice in my head, "That making-decisions deal is fucking hard!" It's safe to say that I was an amateur in this arena back then.

*Decisions can open doors to the unknown.
You decide, and then life will either unfold—
or fold up on your ass.*

In the unfolding of things, life will start to make sense to you and you will realize what no longer serves you. If life decides to fold up on you it may mean that you just might be going the wrong way. But life is funny because no matter if life is *unfolding* or *folding up* there is always a lesson or two stuck between the folds. Along with some spare change and a candy wrapper.

You have to know what feels right to you and be open to developing the ability to first *see yourself as you truly are* so that you can begin to see others as they truly are.

When you decide, you uncover a piece of your power. Some decisions come with more power and awareness, while other decisions may bring you some pain. Either way, feel it and go through it.

When you no longer want to hurt, you just might decide to choose a different course, because the gift of awareness is a gift that keeps on giving.

I knew that I would not be able to grow if I was incapable of making decisions that were in my best interest. And since Will Smith was stressing me out about deciding, I came up with a question that would enable me to get to deciding faster.

The question I asked—and continue to ask— myself is, "Does this work for me?"

There is no right or wrong answer to this question, because the answer will either be yes or no. And regardless of the answer, I follow it with this affirmation/question:

"Everyone else is doing what works best for them, so why should you be any different?"

If the answer is yes, cool; and great for whoever or whatever benefits from your yes, but saying no because you have identified that something doesn't work for you or is not in alignment with where you are going? Now that's powerful.

From personal experience, I have noticed that people hate it when you switch up and start doing what is best for you.

It is usually deemed an expression of selfishness, which is crazy as hell when you think about it. In deciding to choose myself first, I developed the courage to say things like, "Yes, I do have a hundred dollars, but I do not have a hundred dollars to give to you"; "I do have gas in my car, however I do not have time to drive you anywhere."

I used to find these simple truths difficult to say. Setting boundaries in your life can be problematic for many people, and it took me a long time to realize that that was not my problem. I had decided who I was going to be, so I had to set boundaries for what I was willing and able to give to others. In not choosing myself first, I was essentially telling myself that my life and what I was doing was less important than everyone around me.

I now understand why you are to put your oxygen mask on first in the case of an airplane emergency. You cannot help others if you are incapable of being of service to yourself.

You will find that people often expect more from you than they are willing to give themselves, so it's imperative that you don't get caught up in their feelings. We are all responsible for managing our own expectations of others.

> *Expectations are the silent killer,*
> *stay away from them.*

The only person you can control is you.

I found that I could not get people on their *best day* to do for me what I have done for them. Knowing that helps me manage what I expect of others. I have learned that it is easier to just go with my own flow. If people come through for me, that's great, but if they don't I am not moved in any way because I didn't expect anything from them.

Not expecting anything from others helps me to choose me more. It helps me to say yes to myself first.

Decide to save yourself first. This motto and attitude became a part of my 2014 journey.

Here's a little recap:

January 2014

I started with **focus** and made a commitment to end with **boldness**.

There were many busy days and crazy nights, but my fierce

excitement about the journey had me amped up. My focus was different from day to day. I worked to enhance my physical surroundings so I could best tend to my mindset and energy. The first step I took was decluttering my house. I figured I could start with the bare minimum of Feng Shui. Clearing out was really therapeutic. I was at the beginning stage of my commitment, so I had to pour goodness and encouragement into myself, and tell myself all these wonderful things like, "I'm amazing, productive, full of joy, creative and alive, open and unmovable, mindful and in love with life!"

> *I wasn't sure if I could quiet my mind,*
> *so I attended a few meditation classes—*
> *and totally nailed it.*

In creating some empty space in my mind, I was able to daydream about all the things that I desired to attract into my life.

February of 2014

Was crazy-busy. I had just turned 33 years old and things weren't as blissful as compared to January. I was committed to the journey and was still looking forward to the process, but challenges were popping up, and I was only thirty-plus days in. With the emergence of all the challenges, I had the difficult task of adjusting my response to the ebbs and flows of life. **I**

discovered the space in between the different levels of growth. I had to realize that struggle sometimes fills that space, and just because I was struggling did not mean that I was not growing.

This month was all about adjusting and readjusting and reminding myself to do things that were consistent with who I wanted to become. I was frustrated, but **my frustration led me to ask myself the right questions.** By the end of February, I was grateful for the lessons that I had learned and became more willing and open to search for new ways to maximize my efforts going forward.

March of 2014

Started off with me realizing all of my "small moments" because I wanted to make sure that I did not overlook them. **I came up with a series of questions to ensure that my next move or moves were in alignment with the goal that I set**.

The questions were:

"What am I doing?" and "What am I doing it for?"

If I couldn't answer those questions it only meant that I was out of alignment. But the good part was I was open to making the necessary adjustments.

My focus was on positive energy, because I wanted to bring that energy to every speaking engagement, every girls' group, and every art class that I facilitated at schools and churches within the Long Beach community.

Although my focus was "positive energy" there were some negative aspects in my life at that time. For example, I was eating sweets like crazy. Not only did I need to keep my focus on positive energy, I also needed to focus on staying on track. I was seeking positive energy but I was also giving a lot of my energy away.

My energy output was a little out of control because I wanted to help everyone. I finished the month off reminding myself to use my energy in places and with people that appreciated what I had to offer. The more I worked on cultivating my positive energy the more I began to see myself as a great asset to anyone who got the opportunity to be in my space.

I wasn't walking around with my nose in the air, but I was standing a little taller.

Knowing your worth will do that for you.

I had so many desires and ideas which propelled me right into April.

April of 2014

I had an "**I can show you better than I can tell you**" kind of attitude. I was doing it all—wife, mother, sports, appointments, facilitating girls' groups, art classes, and more. I wore myself out a bit, but I was still going strong.

May of 2014

I took some time to look back over the previous months' journal entries and gave myself some words of praise. I was feeling positive and believing in all the good that life had coming my way. But there was **a piece of me that was feeling a bit anxious**. Things were good, but for some reason I wanted things to come faster. I was having some frustrating days. I was trying to stay positive while my days seemed to be getting longer and longer.

I knew I was being pushed towards something bigger, but the waiting was trying to creep in on me as "negative feelings."

But despite all of the mixed feelings I was experiencing, I still had great hope and excitement for my future. I was, however, supposed to be focusing on the little things and little moments in life, anyway.

June of 2014

My life was a little hectic because baseball was still in season and my kids were out of school. Like the previous months, I was looking forward and ready for whatever life wanted to bring my way—**just flowing though the trivial and mundane aspects of life;** kids, life and marriage, and determined not to let any of it get the best of me. **I was fighting to stay positive and productive**.

In the beginning of July 2014

I was still looking for a job. Not because I needed one right away, but because **I had ego issues**. I have always made my own money and brought much to the table, so not having a job was weird as hell.

I was already going through an identity crisis, and not bringing in any money just added to it. The weirdest thing is that I felt like I was robbing my husband every time I swiped my debit card. Therefore, I felt like I had no choice but to put my best foot forward and start job hunting like crazy.

My first job ever was at a credit card company. My friend's mom helped me get the job right out of high school, shortly after I became my own boss. This made my current job hunting an adventure. Not only was it an "adventure" into the unknown—for me; but I had a list of things I was not going to do. For example, working 8 to 5 was on that list. I decided that I would only apply to work for school districts so I could be off at a good time, as well as receive all holidays and vacations. I tested and interviewed, but I guess it was just practice, because I did not get one of those jobs.

At first it was bit frustrating, until I started viewing the job hunt cycle as strictly practice. I started walking into job interviews just as confident as I wanted to be, because I went in knowing I was committed to getting in some practice for the day. Fortunately, practice for me doesn't carry much weight and that made me even more eager to go after what I was truly seeking—whether or not it ended in rejections. I didn't want anyone taking care of me. I loved that I brought money in, and since I wasn't, I struggled with that like crazy.

But there is always something to learn. **I didn't know it would be so hard to allow someone to take care of me.** As I write this today, I want you to know that I am so over that shit. I was tripping. Growth people, it's called growth. Now I'm over here just letting a man be a man.

Being cared for is not that hard after all.

August 2014

Came around and I was in slow motion, so I started to read different books that would enhance my *thought life*. **I was learning to surrender to some things and flow with other things**. August was about owning my journey—and in no particular order.

*Whatever came up I was going
to deal with head on.*

*In doing so, I realized that I could hear
my inner voice more clearly.*

*I was able to recognize when I was playing
on a low energy field and about to nut up.*

I became more aware of the warning signs life sends our way. I was still a little impatient, but I was no longer anxious about what the next chapter in my life would be, and more willing to allow things to *show me* what they were going to be.

September of 2014

Was all about living in the moment and not taking unproductive experiences or thoughts into my next moment. By this time, I was so proud of myself because I was nine months in on the goal that I set. **I wanted my demeanor to speak for me, meaning I had to keep some old behaviors and responses in check**.

By October of 2014

I felt liberated in so many areas of my life. I was conquering a whole bunch of shit and discovering more about myself each day. I was actually practicing patience because I wanted to live my purpose *on purpose* and spend my days doing things that mattered to me. **I made sure that I stayed focused while remaining still.**

My story was developing and I was becoming more aware of that each day.

Each day **I was seeking to learn something new about the world and the role that I played.** I wanted to be alive in all of my moments and love hard in those moments. I was showing up for myself and it felt great.

When November of 2014

Rolled around, I had grown so much. I was reading even more and applying different principles to my life. I was no longer afraid to approach the end of things because I was looking for new beginnings and new insight into everything.

Moral excellence was what I was striving for.

My understanding started to flourish and I was on track to bridging the gap. I was **creatively designing my life and restoring what was lost or misunderstood.**

I was empowered by my own drive, as well as my willingness to journey through some hard lessons. **Reading became my favorite pastime, because gaining knowledge only gave**

me a hunger for more. I believed in my passion and believed with my whole heart that life would give me a great return on my investment. I was grateful for all of the open doors as well as the ones that got slammed in my face. I have to say that I was pretty impressed with myself, and through it all I was seeing nothing but beauty everywhere.

December 2014

Started off great because I considered it my golden month. **I could see the finish line**. I had made a commitment and I was sticking to it—and so very proud of myself for doing so. I was fired up and ready to get through the month so that I could reflect over the whole year.

At this point, I had taught myself how to produce winning thoughts so that I could produce great results. I learned how to be still so that I could hear my inner voice. I learned to detach from things and people that were not aligned with what I wanted and where I was going.

Bottom line: I was just excited!

> *I had decided "what" I was going to be, and "who" I was going to be—and went with it.*

If you're wondering about my best friend who was going to "go on the social media wagon" with me, I have to report that she did not keep her commitment—and any time we talk about goals, I remind her that there is no way in hell that I will make a commitment with her ever again. It's just an ongoing joke that I am never going to let die. But to be totally honest, it didn't matter to me much if my friend came along on this journey, because the truth is—it was one I needed to take alone.

I made an agreement with myself that I would be open to new obstacles and learn my flow in any situation.

I was even willing to go in blind and do things that I was a little afraid to do, just to see where my curiosity would lead me. I decided that I would not give up, and that I was the most important person in my life.

December of 2014 changed my life forever.

But it did not end the way I intended.

CHAPTER 8

FLOAT ON

Reflecting upon the experiences that I documented in my consistent, year-long journaling, I discovered that situations, more often than not, do not unfold within the confines of my pre-conceived notions. Moment by moment, I was learning to accept this reality; you know, just trying to be okay with things. Learning and changing requires a great amount of flexibility, so I was learning each day how to maintain my flow.

I had stretched myself beyond what I thought was possible in 2014, and December was supposed to be THE month I would stamp my personal development passport! (I just made up "personal development passport," but wouldn't it be neat to keep a book full of stamps of events we have traveled through and overcome?) Yes, this was the month that I would give myself an outpouring of words of praise—

celebrating all that I had discovered and worked through during the year. However:

Life is like being out on open water.

At any moment, any situation has the opportunity and ability to change without notice or reason, and the unexpected has the ability to fill me with bouts of uncertainty. Uncertainty is not a feeling I like to experience for very long. It produces in me a nagging desire to hastily get out of the forever-changing water and discover land so that I can stand firmly upon my own two feet.

But discovering land requires time and patience, and becoming hasty adds nothing but layers of stress.

During any self-discovery sojourn, it becomes imperative to learn how to ground yourself; to figure out how to find your footing while doggy paddling around in the emotion ocean. Maintaining foot-composure while drifting in water is not an easy task. It is seemingly downright impossible while the tides come and go, swirling around you.

Consider "mental strength" your floaties.

Only through the development of mental strength are we able to achieve and conquer the task of stabilizing ourselves while adrift. I am not a master, but I have to say that I was getting pretty darn good at it by that point. And yet, my problems do not come on a platter with everything that I need to solve them. My problems are more like a scientific experiment, equipped with instructions that read: *Figure this shit out.*

On December 7, 2014, I received a call in the middle of the night from my dad that left me stranded in the middle of the ocean.

...Do these floaties come in "Jumbo"?

Hours before the call, the Christmas music was blasting and my family and I were decorating our Christmas tree. We went to bed in a jolly, holiday mood. When I answered the phone, my dad spoke words that my heart couldn't comprehend. Those two words turned my life upside down.

"Jared passed."

It was as if life anchored me right then and there. I felt tied down. I was in shock, and rolled out of my bed—allowing my body to fall to the floor. At that moment I got to experience what it is like to feel like you are about to completely lose it. I thought my body was going to shut down. It was cold. I was shaking. And I had the chills for hours. My teeth chattered as if I were standing barefoot in the snow. In the moment, nothing was clicking. I knew I had just heard words that sliced every heart string, but my capability to understand those words was nowhere to be found. I kept asking to be told the story of what happened over and over again because the information would not register fully.

Jared was going to be home on the 13th of December for the graduation party I was throwing for my sister. *Surely this horrible news cannot be real, how could it be?* By this time, I was floating in open water and had totally lost sight of—or the desire for—land. I was unsure of whether I even still had feet to stand upon.

> **All I could do was cry out, on the floor of my bedroom, pleading with the air— "Not my brother! Not my brother!"**

I have five siblings; four of which are the products of my parents, and one half-brother, Jared. I remember it being extremely weird meeting Jared for the first time. I remember thinking to myself, "Who is this kid that keeps telling us, 'I'm going to tell my father'?"

We were looking at him and thinking, "Kid we don't even know you, and we call him 'Daddy,' not 'Father.'"

I cannot even imagine how it must have felt for him. For me, it was a little awkward to meet a sibling that did not live in our same household. I kind of felt sorry for him.

He was quiet, skinny, had asthma, and just a whole bunch of other issues. I did not see him much growing up. We did not discuss him much, either. It was just a known fact that there was another child out there with our last name.

Growing up, Jared's extended family lived on the same block as my grandparents. In high school, his cousin and I became close friends, so I would hear his name from time to time. My dad did not have a relationship with him, and I'm not sure whether he even knew how.

Jared was the product and constant reminder of my dad's reckless times battling drug addiction. My dad was just starting to change when Jared was growing up, and I'm sure that, if he had known how to bring Jared into the equation without disrupting what he was trying to build back up in our family, he would have.

Jared's living conditions were nothing close to how we lived. His home life was full of drugs and everything else that accompanies such a lifestyle. And to top it off, he had to deal with that terrible asthma in an environment that wasn't conducive to his condition.

Years later, I recall getting word that Jared had experienced a horrible asthma attack and was in the hospital, and by this time I was able to go see him on my own. The doctor stated that the asthma attack was so bad, he could have easily died. I remember walking away from his room to the elevator with the image of him all tubed up, weak, and just "out of it," and thinking to myself, "I need to do something."

By the time I got back home, it was clear to me just what I had to do. I figured if no one else was going to look after Jared, then it was up to me.

This decision was not about anyone else. I didn't go to my dad and ask how he would feel. I believe I only mentioned my decision to my sister, who happened to be with me at the time. I was only about 20 years old. I do not know exactly how I even thought up such a grand, life-altering plan, let alone be willing to act on it in real life. But once my mind is set on something there is no turning back. I was only thinking of Jared and his life.

After Jared's grandmother passed away, I made good on my decision. I still had no idea what I was doing. I simply knew my intent was to offer whatever I could in order to give Jared a better quality of life; and if that was with his 21-year-old sister who thought she had life figured out, then so be it. His mother didn't give me any problems when I went to get him. She loved him and knew it was best for him. He was my brother, and although I did not know him well, I refused to stand by and let him die.

I enrolled him in school. I was present at his school events. I checked his grades, developed a rapport with his teachers, and provided him with everything that he needed to excel in school and in life. His interests and hobbies changed often. One day he was a skateboarder and then the next I was purchasing a guitar because, out of nowhere, he was now a "guitar player."

I just wanted him to have a fair shot at life.

Sister Mom. I know it was hard for him, because it's difficult being an outsider, and even harder when you *feel* like one. I quickly went from simply being his sister to taking on the role and responsibilities of being his mother/sister.

Jared was a great kid. He was only problematic when it came to his art classes and art teachers. He was naturally gifted and could draw like no other. He was self-taught.

When he was young and the adults in his environment were doing what they did, he would sit for hours tracing comic books.

By the time he entered high school, Jared figured his teachers didn't know shit—and could neither teach him shit—about art, and consequently, he gave himself permission to disregard the instructions for his assignments.

Besides his light rebellion in art class, he was easy; only asking for what he needed—which made him so super easy to love. If he only needed fifty cents, he would ask for no more and no less. It was the craziest thing. I would look at him and say, "Don't you just want a dollar?" Nonetheless, he only needed what he needed.

My mother gave me hell for my decision. I am sure my decision concerned her a bit, considering I was in my early twenties taking care of a 15-year-old. My caring for him and having him in her everyday life brought back a flood of painful emotions that she had buried long ago. Having reached adulthood, I can now understand her pain. Deep-rooted pain is hard to deal with, I get it. But it does not go away until we stop avoiding it and actually just deal with it. In no way did I want to project pain onto my mother. She has dealt with enough pain in her life. But there was no other way I could have gone about this. I had to do what was on my heart.

My decision to take Jared under my wing was not based off of some need to right the wrongs in my dad's life. I did it simply because someone needed to.

And so, emotions were raging, and I was caught in the crossfire and took many shots. I wanted to protect him from feeling unwanted and from all the drama and tension that came with my decision. My mother's pain did not make that an easy task, and my dad didn't have a clue what to do. But Jared needed someone, and it just so happened that he had a somebody like me as his sister.

In time and with time, things did start to get better. It took my mom some time, but she started to come around. The first couple of holiday dinners were weird, but we got through them. I remained sister/mom for a long time, but gradually I began to observe a shift in our dynamic. Jared moved in with my parents following the birth of my first child.

Everyone, including Jared, was working through various emotions, but harmony was on the horizon.

Jared graduated from high school and found a completely different path to walk in life compared to his life in the past. He was a true artist—creative, and totally outside of the box.

He was so outside of the box that he married a Bulgarian girl after knowing her for only two months.

Now, I love her to pieces, but when he initially called to tell me that he had married what was essentially a stranger, I wanted to kill him. But by this time, I knew he was a free spirit. So when he told me things like, "I quit my job today," I was not at all surprised or moved. However, I did inform him that, in this case, this was a *marriage*, not a job at Jamba Juice he could just quit because he no longer felt like working there. This was real life! Looking back, she was the greatest gift to him. They moved to San Francisco to pursue art degrees at the Academy of Art University.

I was such a proud sister/mom. Though, by this time, I was just his sister, because he was calling my mom for all of the life advice. And she was laying advice on him as if she had birthed him herself. In simple terms, he was getting his ass cussed out just like everyone else. I know this sounds funny, but there was so much beauty in that, because it was an indication that she looked at him as one of her own and had no problem checking his ass.

It was amazing to witness them turn pain and turmoil into a powerful union of love.

Life is crazy. We never know what life will bring our way, or how it will be packaged. My decision kind of pushed my mother towards her pain and although it was packaged that way, she unwrapped more joy than she could possibly imagine for herself in this situation. Once she was willing to work through some things, her capacity to love grew greater.

What I did for my brother continues to be a decision I am most proud of in my life. He is for sure one of my greatest accomplishments.

When I think of him, I am reminded of how I want to show up in the world each and every day.

I am empowered by how effortlessly I made the decision to care for and to love him. I had a thought, put some action behind that thought, and ultimately changed the course of his life.

On December 14, 2014, I wrote about the healing Jared brought to our family. I was trying really hard to stay in a positive space and remain "lifted" because I had to handle things for a funeral I didn't even want to attend. Saying goodbye that soon was not how I saw this working out in my head.

> *Like a mother has dreams for her kids,*
> *I had dreams for my brother.*
> *Dreams full of vibrant color and life.*

We laid Jared to rest on December 18, 2014, in a sweater, jeans, and some Vans. The whole "suit" thing would have been too weird. My life and everything about me changed following Jared's arrival and departure from my life. I had been on a journey of discovering myself that whole year, but felt totally lost at that point.

On December 31, 2014, I wrote:

> *I was really looking forward to this day. I just had no idea what would take place before getting here. The year was good to me and I had a lot of happy moments and a lot of growth. I'm so proud of myself for keeping my commitment. My year*

is ending without my brother and that is taking so much out of me. I'm trying to focus, trying to learn and continue to grow, but I am having such a hard time. I know I will get through this because I have hope; but "How am I going to get through this?" is the question. This day has really been a lot emotionally, but I am looking forward to better days. Rest in peace, Jared, I love you to pieces. I will miss your presence, but I will carry you in my spirit. I love you, and in 2015, I will honor your life by living mine. There was nothing I wouldn't do for you. There was nothing I wouldn't give for your happiness. I will honor you, and since you can't live this life, I'll be alive enough for the both of us.

I'll fly because I still have wings.

All of that sure did look good on paper. However, I was numb and out of it. I couldn't even feel my "wings."

I continued to journal because I was trying my hardest not to dive into a full-blown depression. The start of 2015 was the worst time of my life. On January 12, 2015, Jared's death certificate arrived in the mail.

At the age of 27, my baby brother passed away from a severe asthma attack.

I was so angry, because I just did not get it. He died from the very thing I thought I was saving him from. He was just starting to live and find his way, and was blossoming into the tattoo business and really honing in on his craft.

"Gone too soon" is a catchy phrase, but that did not cover the emotion that accompanies such a loss. Life just left me disoriented, and I was trying to fight off every thought and feeling that was making me feel terrible, but nothing was moving.

I knew what it felt like to dream, be happy, and have the ability to pick myself back up; I just couldn't do it. I was too fucking broken, and too damn sad. I was grateful that I was still living—I just didn't feel alive. Jared's death dimmed my light. I did want to feel different, because I wanted the passion and drive back that I had been nurturing all year long, but I couldn't seem to reach it. A part of me desired to make a new agreement with myself and pick myself up but nothing was sticking.

On February 17, 2015, I wrote:

I'm ready to get back to me
Ready, but I have this pull on me
I'm in a stage of disbelief
I know my passion exists
I just can't feel it
I can't feel the sun
Butterflies are colorless

The scent of roses is gone
I'm stuck between two worlds
I'm in the world of nothingness
I can't feel
I can't see
I can't hear
I'm missing the signs
Not even sure if they're there
I know my passion
I remember how it feels
But I can't get past
I can't break through
I'm lost because of my loss
And I don't know what to do
I can't feel the wind
I can't hear the waves
My view of life has changed
I long for colors to fill my eyes
But all this hurt is blocking all I have inside.

I was a mess and I never, ever thought in a million years that I would come to appreciate my tears. I know it sounds a little crazy, but I couldn't imagine having all this hurt inside of me and having a dry cry. I cried so many tears. Turns out that I have an unlimited amount of this salty liquid, but I thank God for the endless supply.

I am also grateful for Hershey Kisses and Netflix.

Whoever is the CEO of Netflix, I just want to say, I love you. Without the combination of Hershey Kisses and Netflix, this girl would surely have gone crazy. I know my choices are not on the list of the healthiest things to indulge in, but my grief called for plenty of chocolate and endless entertainment.

Don't judge me.

To my surprise, I continued to journal each day. I journaled even if I didn't have much to say. On those days, my journal entries read in big letters, "I don't have anything to say."

On March 16, 2015, I wrote:

"Take control of your life, because you are losing it."

And to be honest, I was. I totally forgot how to cook; there were times that I couldn't put one meal together. But even though I was kind of losing my grip on life, I still tried my hardest to keep going. I was hurt and broken, but I was also ready to feel something again. Loving my brother was such a privilege, and I had too much to offer life to stay stuck.

I was aware of the days, because I was counting them like crazy and driving myself crazy. I didn't have normal days. Each day was just another day added to the count of days since I lost my brother. The 7th of each month was horrible for me. Eventually, I decided to do something about it.

When the 7th would approach, I would float my dreams.

Meaning, I would do something, anything, to keep my dreams above water.

I decided to do seven things on the 7th of each month that would get me closer to my dreams or just simply make me happy in the moment. They were simple things, such as: eating ice cream, going to the beach, or sending seven handwritten notes to whomever.

My focus on the 7th of each month went from focusing on my brother's death to focusing on getting the seven things done. I didn't mind driving 40 blocks down to the beach just to hear the waves, then checking that off my list for the day. It was just a way to focus my energy on something besides sadness and loss, and it worked.

Before I knew it, the 7th of each month took on a different meaning for me; and eventually, I stopped counting.

97

In July of 2015, I started to doodle my dreams. I began to draw everything that I wanted to manifest in my life. Stick figures and all, I was a doodling fool.

All the drawing helped me; shit, I think it saved me. I would draw an airplane that represented family vacations I wanted to go on. I would draw a bank receipt showing plenty of zeros in my bank account. But the most important drawing was the one of me laying by my brother's grave with a smile on my face, because I had found some peace.

Losing my brother derailed me, but somehow, someway, I started finding my way back. I missed him dearly. And I still have my days where I am flooded with the reality of my loss, and I feel as if I cannot breathe. My sisters and brother lost a brother, but, like my parents, I feel like I lost a son.

As tough as it was, I didn't realize at the time that every time I was willing to journal or draw or do something that made me happy—no matter how small—I was clearing a path for light to get through.

The struggle of trying to get back to myself through all the pain made me stronger.

Although December of 2014 turned out to be the worst month of my life, I now know that when your heart is broken wide open you have no choice but to let the light in. I learned that a blank canvas will not remain blank for very long if, in time, and when it is time, you grip the paintbrush and just fucking paint.

When I did, I discovered that the paintbrush had never even left my hand.

CHAPTER 9

ATTITUDE IS EVERYTHING

After some time feeling spiritually and physically stuck, I recalibrated my desire to be more and become more, which prompted me to make some moves. I was ready to act and move my life forward. "Coming into being" was a craving that I could neither ignore nor deny—no matter what I had gone through. A sense of self-control was emerging while I simultaneously began to understand more and more about "life." After grappling with reality and my life experiences, the path that I needed to follow was becoming clearer. I could now see miles down the road.

Though my mental state ebbed and flowed, I fought like crazy to return to my authentic self, my authentic drive, and to not only *return* to self, but to emerge greater than before. I was met with many detours on this road, but was no longer afraid.

I knew that pain brought pressure, and that heartache often decreases joy, but *not living* just so I could avoid the two extremes wasn't something I was willing to do anymore.

There were countless times when the light of my path grew dark and uncertain, but I was more eager to follow through with my journey than worry about issues with the lighting.

We are all living this life of no guarantees, so I made the conscious choice to get out of my comfort zone, just strap on that "third eye chakra headlamp" and plow ahead.

At times, sitting still and allowing myself to feel was all that I needed in order to break through and achieve self-actualization. I adopted a "born again" attitude, because it is the perspective that we choose throughout our journey that ultimately directs our path.

Perspective is everything.

It literally creates the reality in which we choose to live.

**Most situations in life will offer at least three perspec-
tives:** one that focuses on the problem at hand, the other focusing
on the knowledge inherently gained as a result of the problem,
and one that is somewhere in between. Let my husband tell it, I
linger on the side that focuses on the problem. And maybe I am
guilty of this from time to time, but I'm growing and becoming
more aware of how I move in my everyday life.

From my perspective, I am "working through the problem to
gain knowledge and, in order to work through it, I have to bring
the problem up again and again."

It's just how I work through things, and it drives my husband
insane.

The bottom line is that we get to choose the route we take to
gaining perspective. In "perspective" there is either something
lost, something to gain, or something that needs to be discovered
or approached in a different way. You just have to choose your
mindset. Looking at any situation and trying to gain insight and
respond accordingly can be tough, but someone has to do it. Might
as well be you!

For me, maintaining a positive perspective on life is something
that requires consistent attention and redirection. Sometimes, I
am a little off and the negative aspects of my attitude completely
take over. This negativity then clouds my judgment and, in those
moments, I am only able to focus on what I deem to be "bad" in these
predicaments. (But we don't need to let my husband know that.)

Lucky for me, life is always giving me an opportunity to take on a fresh perspective, and sometimes, adopt a new motto...

The pieces to our stories can be found anywhere.

I just happened to find a little nugget of my story when my dad was telling his own story.

It was around 10:00 p.m. on a Tuesday in the middle of August. I was exhausted, but I couldn't go to sleep because I had to pick my parents up from the airport. I knew that if I were to lie down and allow myself to "rest" for an hour and a half, I was guaranteed to wake up with a bad attitude. I'm the type of person who battles with midday naps or short naps. I can't simply "catch a little shut eye" in the middle of the day, because it somehow always turns into me waking up on the wrong side of the bed—no "refreshed," or "peachy" feelings involved.

If I am relaxing at home and my husband sees that I am about to fall asleep in the middle of the day, he may say,

"Please don't do it, you know how you get."

103

Of course, I take zero ownership in this situation. As a matter of fact, I act like I have no idea what he is talking about. Sure, we all know "that someone" who can fall asleep anywhere. Sitting upright, on a plane, in a car... Oh, the nerve. And it is never a light sleep: they are mouth-open, drool flowing, eyelids twitching, *knocked out.* I envy those people because that is something that I am incapable of achieving; even when I was pregnant.

Moral of the story is, I try to stay away from the short naps that others swear to be so recharging and rejuvenating. (If you are one of those people just know that I am rolling my eyes at you right now.) Because of this, I made the decision to just stay up since their flight didn't get in until 11:45 p.m.

After all of that, can you guess what I did?

Yes. I set my alarm to sound after an hour and a half, and then drifted off to sleep. An hour into my slumber, my older sister called. Though I was not in a *deep* sleep, the ringing of my phone scared the shit out of me. My heart was beating rapidly. My first and only thought was that I had overslept. I managed to say, "Hello?!" and my sister immediately began talking my ear off.

It was about 11:00 p.m., she was wide awake, and loud as hell.

This was my reminder call. Though it was jarring, it was effective; I was awake indeed. I turned over and looked at my husband asleep. And I really wanted to strongly suggest to him that *he* should go pick my parents up, but he had just worked a 24-hour shift. Though it was tempting to just wake him up and have him go, that would have been plain selfish on my part. I would have said something along the lines of, "What kind of man would want their beautiful, sleepy wife driving to the airport?"

But I did not do it. Not because of any moral superiority on my part; rather, because my sister-in-law had already volunteered to ride with me, so he was in the clear. I rolled myself out of bed, put my jacket and shoes on, grabbed a handful of Fruit Loops and headed out the door.

It did not occur to me to check their flight status. I just figured that since they were not flying in from San Francisco, there would be no delays. (While I am on the topic, I think it's fitting to mention that I never plan to fly in or out of San Francisco because the fog tries to hold you hostage and the delays make no sense.) Leaving the house, my only concern was being on time because my dad is such a punctual person, and I knew that it would have driven him crazy if he had to wait to be picked up.

Allow me to back up. My parents and I had planned their trip transportation itinerary the day before they were to leave. Firstly, they needed to be at the airport by 9:00 p.m. It was an international flight, and they needed to be there three hours prior to take-off. They were coming from their home in Riverside, which is a forty-five-minute drive from Long Beach on a good day. They were to pick me up from my house so that I could, in turn, drive them in their car to LAX, allowing me to bring their car back to my house while they were out of town.

On the day of departure, my parents arrived at my house around 9:05 p.m. We were thinking, "No problem; the airport is only twenty minutes away." My parents, my husband, and I swiftly hopped into their car. My husband had accompanied me on that ride because, "What kind of man would want their beautiful wife driving at night?"

A little manipulative, I know.

But I do not recall the title of this book reading, "Perfect Little Me." Moving on...

We merged onto the I-405 freeway, and traffic was at a complete standstill. I could sense that my dad wanted to lose his mind; but instead he opted to lightly strike the steering wheel. I am certain that he wanted to rip the steering wheel from the dashboard and chuck it through the windshield. Alternately, he chose to mutter under his breath, "I knew it, I knew it. I would have already been at the airport if it was just me." My mom paid him no mind because she is always late; and by the grace of God, things somehow always come together. (Herein lies an example of maintaining a positive attitude and perspective, and trusting your path in life's journey.)

Internally, my dad was boiling, because this is not how he gets down. My dad is the guy who shows up an hour before he is scheduled to begin his shift at work. Though he remained relatively silent during the drive, I know that he had a million things that he wished to say to my mom. All the while, I was silently cracking up. If he had chosen to speak, he would have said something along the lines of, "When I die, just start the funeral; your mom is going to be late either way."

He would have followed it up by hypothetically asking, "Why would a person make a hair appointment in Long Beach, on the day of their trip, just to drive back to Riverside to pack their bags, only to drive right back to Long Beach, to drive straight to LAX? Why?" I am sure that my dad wanted to go crazy. (This is a side note, but my mom *was* still getting her hair done in Long Beach when she was supposed to be home in Riverside packing the rest of her stuff.)

I am sure my dad wanted to get out
of the car, stand in the middle of traffic
with arms outstretched, and scream, "Why?!"
with eyes searching the sky, pleading with
God to provide him with an answer.

But my dad is smart. He was not trying to rock my mom's boat and piss her off—only to sit alongside her on a long, international flight. Needless to say, he kept his complaints to a minimum. I dropped my parents off at the airport around 9:40 p.m., and they made it to their gate and boarded their flight without a hitch.

Their return flight was supposed to come in at 11:45 p.m., but it was delayed. I could have checked their flight status before leaving home, but as aforementioned, I figured that since they weren't coming in from San Francisco, their flight would arrive in a timely manner. (Small-picture thinking, but, hey.)

To avoid circling the airport multiple times, I decided to wait in the Marriott parking lot down the street. Their flight landed at 12:10 a.m., and they were ready for me to provide curbside service at around 12:40 a.m. They got into the car and immediately began talking about the amazing time they had while vacationing in Jamaica. They were so impressed with how hard working the natives of Jamaica were. They spoke highly of the service that they received, and the laid back "no worry" attitude adopted by the people. My dad told a story about my mom getting stopped while going through customs because she had a mango in her purse. My dad had given it to her the previous day, and she completely forgot about it. She is now known as the Mango Smuggler.

He proceeded to describe the manner in which the Jamaicans drive, speak, and of course how wonderful and tasty the jerk chicken was. I was intrigued by each story and passionate recount that flew from my parents' lips.

But there was one story that heavily resonated with me. It was the story about a bus driver who told them, "We don't have problems, mon'. Just situations." I repeated the phrase multiple times in my head to ensure that the exact words and message would remain with me upon waking the next morning.

"We don't have problems, just situations."

This arrangement of words spoke intensely to my internal self. In that moment, however, I was unsure of how to apply it to my life. Fortunately, "uncertainty" had become the catalyst that fueled my search for answers; it was no longer my greatest fear. I wanted to "connect" and gain a deeper understanding of that bus driver's words.

In short—this was some deep shit.

When a situation unfolds in a way that leads us to believe that a problem has risen, we give power to the word "problem." At the conclusion of deeming something as a problem, we literally *create* the problem. Our thoughts and words carry energy. If we believe something to be true, then it is true. Therefore, if one holds the belief that they are not good enough, then they, in fact, are not good enough.

Contemplate the following phrases:

"I was just minding my own business; but no matter what I do, trouble seems to follow me."

"'Problems' is my middle name."

"I can't get ahead in life because bad things always happen to me."

"My life is hard."

"Just my luck..."

Energy is omniscient, omnipotent, and omnipresent.

It is free flowing.

Energy is capable of flowing in any direction at any given moment. It is a collector of thoughts—and it has no bias. Therefore, "Energy" has no concept or reason to create a distinction between which thoughts to collect or abandon.

All thoughts are caught in Energy's net.

Energy's sole function is to transform our thoughts into reality.

Perception is akin to "life energy." Perception is the means through which we process the world. And because perception carries energy, whatever we think or feel to be true, in turn, shapes that reality.

If you think you have problems, guess what my friend, you have got problems. The word "**problem**" carries so much weight. It is fueled by uncertainty and anxiety.

If Energy could send a memo it would read as follows:

Dear _____,

My only job is to flow. I do not have time to hold your hand through life, or coach you on "how to think" or "feel" about what you *think* you know. My job is to turn thoughts into reality. That's all I'm getting paid for.

Therefore, if you think you have problems in your life, my job is to transform your thoughts into reality. I create the problems that your thoughts demand. You're welcome.

In closing, be mindful of the power of your thoughts.

Sincerely,
Energy

I currently work at my children's middle school, and on most days, I am outside walking around. I would not consider myself to be an outdoor person, mostly due to the fact that I cannot stand bugs, and I am terrified of bees, which is problematic.

I use the word "problematic" because the influx of bees in my vicinity, indeed, presented me with a problem. I know, I know, I just gave a whole run down on thoughts, but just follow me. I am terrified of bees because I just *know* that if they are around, I am going to get stung.

Whether rational or not, my conclusion is solidified. The presence of more bees meant that it was more than likely that I would receive an unwarranted sting by one of those tiny bastards. I am the type of person who could be talking to someone, see a bee fly by, and out of pure instinct I begin fighting the air, ducking, or take off running. Usually, I leave the other person standing there unaware of what is going on, looking at me like I am crazy because they never even saw the bee.

This zany display is usually accompanied by them asking, "Are you allergic to bees?" I fear answering this question, because my response is typically a whisper of, "I don't know. I have never been stung."

But I am positive that if I ever were stung, I would be acting so crazy, that one would think I was allergic.

112

Though it may sound irrational, or possibly insane, this is my reality. There were bees everywhere on campus, and it just so happened that wherever I happened to be, the bees were soon to follow. Imagine these bees spending their entire day following me. And therein lies the power of thought.

The campus is fairly large, so I usually use a golf cart to get from point A to point B. I remember being in the front of the school in the middle of the parking lot one day when a bee decided to pay me a visit. I was the only faculty member supervising that area at the time, so if anyone witnessed this situation, I'm sure they thought I was just a little on the crazy side. Upon the bee's arrival, I jumped out of the cart while waving and fighting the air.

I pulled off my jacket in a full panic, thinking that the bee had landed on me. Without hesitation, I abandoned that cart right in the middle of the parking lot.

I am very dramatic, so I am certain that I caused quite the scene. If it were up to me, I would have left that damn bee-attracting cart there for eternity. But I had enough clarity of mind to wonder how dumb my answer would sound when my boss radioed me to inquire about the traffic-blocking golf cart, so I paused.

Hoping that the bee had flown away, I mustered up the bravery to slowly approach the cart and drive to another area on campus.

But can you guess what was following me? Yet another damn bee.

At this point I was on the verge of losing my mind. (And I'm still not entirely convinced that bees have anything to do with making honey. Come on, now. There was zero evidence of honey production going on in the parking lot of our middle school that I could see.)

I called my husband to let him know: "If a bee stings me, I am quitting my job."

A bit extreme, I know; but I was so serious.

Let me not lose focus here: This story is being told to exemplify the power of the energy that lives within our thoughts and perception.

"I fear receiving a sting by one of these bees," is what I put out into the world.

Thoughts carry energy. Energy transforms thoughts into reality. If I control my thoughts, and energy transforms my thoughts into reality, then, deductively, I am in complete control of my reality.

"We don't have problems, just situations."

This profound statement made by my parents' Jamaican holiday bus driver resonated through every fiber of my being. I began to focus on the power that I held over creating my reality. I became aware of my habitual statements, such as, "No matter what, bees find me. I will bet anything that I get stung by one of these bees." I classified the bees' presence in my life as a problem based on my fear of getting stung. My fear and my thoughts gave Energy permission to create a fear-based reality in regard to the "bee presence" in my life.

The truth, however, is that bees are not the least bit concerned with me.

I know that I am important, but I am more than certain that local bee colonies are not holding morning meetings solely focused on creative and trendy ways to fly by me just to mess up my day.

I like to think that they simply assume that I am a flower; and when they discover that I am not, they naturally move on. I created the thought that birthed the energy that shaped a reality in which bees were drawn to me with the sole purpose of driving their stingers into my flesh. I now realize my energy caused their attraction: I attracted the bees to me.

Shoot.

I still walk around campus, and, like any other day, there are bees flying around. *However, the moment that I stopped worrying about them, they magically stopped paying me visits.* I constantly reassure myself that I did not serve a purpose in their "busy bee" life.

Our thoughts hold power in the sense that they inherently carry and/or produce energy. Energy freely flows in any and all directions. Energy's sole purpose is to collect any and all thoughts and transform them into reality.

Your life is an echo of where and how you choose to focus your energy.

I feared being stung by the bees. But the bees were never the problem; they were simply completing the work set out for a bee. They were doing their job. The situation was that it was spring; and spring is the exact time that one would expect to encounter a swarm of bees. Their heightened presence in my life was not a guarantee that I was destined to be stung. My fear, frustration, and anxiety could have been eased if I had chosen not to give in to my fear-driven thoughts. I created a problem where there was none.

At the time, I was unaware that I had the choice to simply view it as a *situation*, as opposed to seeing it as a major *problem*. With the knowledge that I now possess, I realize that those bee-laden workdays could have been much more pleasant for me. (Now, I wonder what would happen if my dad were to apply this same philosophy to the issue he has with my mom always running late!)

"No problems, mon! Only situations."

Go paint THAT somewhere.

CHAPTER 10

THE HORSE WITH NO NAME

Fuck it.

"Fuck it" is an expression. It is an *attitude* word. When I use the word fuck, it enables me to get my point across using fewer words. Of course, I use it when I am frustrated. The "Fuck!" that I use when I am frustrated holds a different connotation than the "Fuck it!" that I am going to explain here.

"Fuck it," for me, is a call to action.

It is a declarative statement that I use to propel myself forward in life. It's akin to saying, "Let's do this!" "You've got this!" "I am all in!" "I am fearless!" "Seize the day!"

There are moments in our lives when we are afraid to take the next step. We freeze. And to quickly build up our courage we need strong words that will help move and guide us in the appropriate direction. Well, "fuck it" are my words of choice. Saying, "Okay, fuck it, I'm in," perpetuates the courage I need in moments to do something brave—like stepping outside my comfort zone.

> *It stirs up in me the "What've I got to lose?" feeling; it channels my inner Braveheart, or Foxy Brown.*

In saying fuck it, I step in front of fear and doubt. With fear and doubt relegated to the sideline I am ready to conquer whatever may lie ahead. I have the perfect example of a *"fuck it"* situation that took place when my husband and I went horseback riding four years ago.

My husband had arranged a "just because" trip. We drove about four and a half hours from our home to Pismo Beach, California. He had something planned for us to do each day. And I really enjoyed every part of it; especially the part where he wanted to keep me blindfolded for the entire ride up! (He didn't think that part through, but I've got to love him for trying.) He planned for us to go horseback riding—and I have to be honest here—I was a little apprehensive due to my fear of the unknown. This would be my first time going horseback riding. I've sat on a pony before as a kid, but that is it. Everything that I could possibly be afraid of came to mind. Bugs, nature, losing control, my horse just running off at full speed; and who knows what else. I'm sure you would agree that there was plenty to be afraid of, right?

On one hand I was scared; but on the other, I was given the opportunity to ride a horse, down a beautiful beach, at sunset. I mean come on, how perfect is that?

This situation—a combination of fear, apprehension, awareness, and the foresight to trust the journey of the unknown—culminated into a classic "fuck it" scenario.

And that is exactly how I responded. I said, fuck it, and decided to join my husband, the guide, and the rest of the group on this horseback-riding excursion. Saying "fuck it" provided me with the courage I needed to take the first steps into accepting and inviting this experience into my life. There was no guarantee that this excursion would run smoothly and safely. For instance, I had no idea that we would have to go through the jungle to actually get to the damn beach.

Accepting the "journey into the unknown" was one thing; riding through the jungle was not what I signed up for.

All I wanted was to get to the place that they displayed in the damn advertisement. I wanted to be *on the beach*, and ride a horse that walks in a straight line, following the butt of the horse preceding it. Going through the woods and sand dunes to experience the beach sunset was *not* on my list.

Agreeing to place myself into this terrifying situation was all that plagued my mind. I kept thinking, "I am on a horse, and my biggest fear is that my feet cannot touch the ground. I am in nature—the wild—surrounded by bushes, trees, and flowers."

Do you know what loves bushes, trees, and flowers? Bees. Bees love those things. Wherever nature goes, bees will follow. Though I was now able to comprehend the fact that the bees were not concerned with me, per se, I remained steadfast in my belief that it was not the day for one of those bastards to land on me.

Our guide was yelling out a plethora of instructions in an effort to get us to effectively ride and guide our horses. Our guide's name was Amy. And Amy's instructions included, but were not limited to, "Do this!" "Pull up like this," "Pull left if you want your horse to go right," "Pull right if you want your horse to go left." I was overwhelmed with confusion, and thinking: *What? Wait a minute. I am not ready—I am confused.*

Besides the bees, random bugs were flying around in every direction. The start to my horseback riding adventure was a little terrifying. My horse appeared fickle, yet incessantly focused on killing me in some fashion. We were traveling down a narrow trail, and my horse insisted upon walking right alongside the edge. Life, for me, was about to be over, but I could not shake the possibility of a bee (or any bug) entering my space and not being able to run.

I was fully exposed and defenseless.

I know NOW that the actions of my horse were a direct response to the fear, confusion, and insecurity that I was feeling in my role "guiding and leading" it down the trail that we were on. But I was incapable of using my body to direct the horse (properly). I was frozen. My left leg was sticking straight out because I was terrified. I could not loosen up enough to implement the instructions given by the guide, or bend my leg normally.

Let me tell it, my horse was out of control and had a mind of its own. My hands were fully occupied because I was *attempting* to control this rabid horse, so of course I would be rendered helpless if a bee, a bird, or anything with wings decided to come near me. I know what I do when I'm on foot and a bug comes buzzing. But being on a horse? I am almost certain I would fall off the horse trying to dodge the flying insects—and thus break my own damn neck.

Logical maybe not, but this is me we are talking about. If I shared these feelings with my family they would say that it sounds about right; considering they have seen me go crazy over flies. Anyways, I know I am saying a lot, because I really want you to get how uncomfortable and worried I was about this experience! Match me in my anxiety, if you will.

As discussed in the previous chapter, if you think you have problems, then a problematic situation is exactly what you will manifest.

Thinking that I would break my neck by falling off of my horse in an attempt to dodge any and all flying specimens, I was focusing my energy on the possibility that this exact situation would arise.

Energy, in all of its forms, is simply another term for power.

For instance, if you focus on not stuttering while speaking, the chances of you stumbling over a word are instantly increased. Though I was privy to this theory, I could not force myself to calm my mind of negative thoughts in that moment. The fact of the matter was that I was scared and uncomfortable due to the various unknown factors at play.

There were eight other people embarking on this excursion, and our guide, Amy, was riding six horses ahead of me. My fear and lack of confidence made me feel like she was riding five miles ahead. The entire time I was yelling: "Excuse me! My horse is really close to the edge. Excuse me!" The quivering of my vocal chords forced my words to shake their way out of my throat chakra. I pulled back to regain control over my horse, but he was insistent upon walking right against the trail edge.

Little did I know, it was my "stiff-leg-sticking-out-to-the-side" and the manner in which I was holding the reins that was the exact reason why my horse was so confused. My fear-fueled awkwardness was like a moth to flame. Unknowingly, I was in complete control and the sole reason why my horse kept trying to kill me.

Upon exiting the jungle and arriving at the beach, I was able to breathe again. My leg (and I) eventually relaxed; and my love of the beach allowed me to enjoy the moment and focus on the sound of the waves crashing against the shore. Finally feeling safe, I thought: "Now this is what I'm talking about!"

With my newfound sense of serenity, I looked back at my husband and asked that he take my picture. Usually, I am the selfie queen, but there was no way in hell that I was letting go of that horse.

In that moment, my "fuck it" decision from the outset felt very well made. I had reached the finish line! I was at ease and felt accomplished thinking that I had made it to the end. I had made it to the beach. There would be no more trekking up and down the mountainside; no more bee-riddled bushes. There was just sand, water, and waves, and I was basking in the feeling of gratefulness.

Persevering to the end was worth all of the pushing that it took for me to continue, because—surprise, surprise—there had been many times I wanted to ask to be let off *that* rollercoaster.

Enjoying the beach, I really didn't give much thought to the route that we would need to take in order to get *back* to the ranch. Maybe they had a team of people that took the horses back to the ranch. Either way, that certainly wasn't my concern.

Unfortunately, that turned out to be wishful thinking (and hoping) on my part. We had been given a glimpse of paradise, simply to be required to retrace our steps back to the start line?!

My "Fuck it!" attitude quickly transformed into a dreadful, "Oh, fuck."

We began the journey back through the sand dunes, which were not half bad, until we entered an unknown area of the jungle. (I live in the city, so my perspective of what defines a "jungle" may have been a bit exaggerated. Basically, I would consider a field of overgrown orange trees to be a jungle.)

I soon realized that the trip back was much worse.

The return trail was quite narrow, with hardly enough room to fit a horse. Branches and bushes were sticking out every which way, causing me to obsess over the possibility of coming in contact with poison ivy...and bees. The "poison ivy" idea comes from movies I have seen where people just run into the woods, but I have no idea whether they are actually running through poison ivy or not.

We ducked and dodged as we went along, trying to avoid getting our eyes poked out by the tree branches. And let me not forget my dear old horse, who now decided to *run* whenever he saw fit.

Reminiscent of a young child on a road trip, I kept screaming to our guide Amy, "Are we there yet?"

"How Much longer?"

"Where do we have to go?"

"My horse keeps running by himself!"

"...Are we almost there?"

Honestly, if I had known what I would have to ride through to get to the beach, I probably would have passed on the entire opportunity. I was, however, relieved and extremely proud of myself when we finally reached the ranch. With ego and arrogance aside—I swear—I acknowledged and congratulated myself for all the strength that it took for me to see the journey to fruition.

Was I scared? Yes. I did, however, persevere. I survived a situation wherein I failed to have even *minimal* control over the outcome. My feet were not even touching the ground—yet I made a choice to keep going amid fear surrounding me on all sides. Who knew that once I got on that horse, there was no turning back?

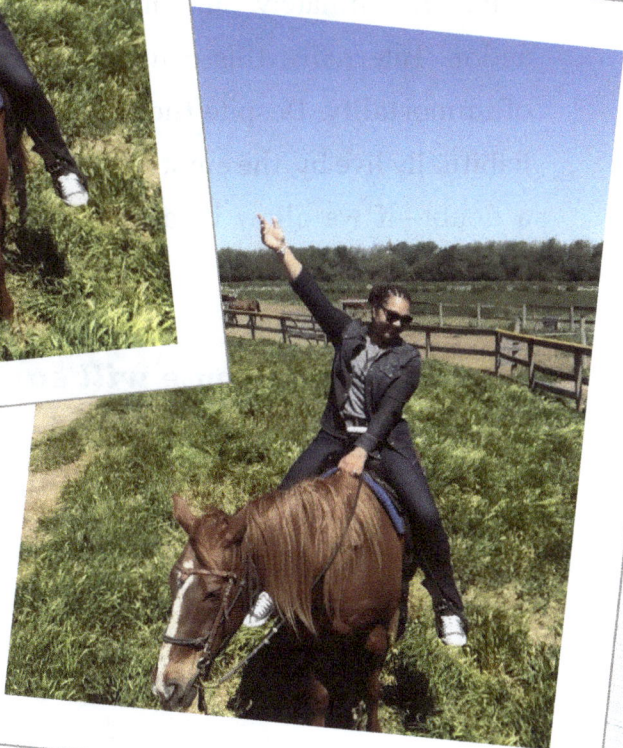

That horseback riding expedition was the experience of a lifetime, which would have been impossible without my "fuck it" attitude.

My mindset enabled, supported, and filled me with the courage (and, in retrospect, humor) that allowed me to acknowledge and face my fears, doing something I could not normally do.

Simply, *"fuck it"* is an attitude. It is a choice that holds the power to fill the well of courage that resides in my soul. Saying "Fuck it!" innately supports and fuels me to respond with action. Internally, this courageousness gives rise to the feeling of immortality. Despite the levels or depths of fear that we may habitually live by, the emotional presence of courage will, without a doubt—if we allow it—always surmount our insecurities and apprehensions.

Just as some will say that "fear is what keeps us alive," I say that courage is what makes us thrive.

This is the part where I bring it all together to encourage YOU to say "fuck it" and paint YOUR story. Painting, both figuratively and literally, is the moment when the mess transcends into magic. Deciding to paint ensures that you will do it. It means that, not only are you ready to tackle what you already know lies ahead, but that you welcome and are willing to conquer the unknown. It means that you get to choose the colors that will inevitably transform your blank canvas into a masterpiece of your dreams.

You should feel fear when tackling a new task.

If you do not feel an inkling of uncertainty Day One of going after your dreams, if your heart is not racing while making an important decision, then what you are seeking is too small.

I made it back to the ranch in one piece. I let go of the reins on that horse, put my hands in the air, and told my husband to snap a picture.

(Quickly.)

Now is the time to say *fuck it,* and paint as boldly as you possibly can!

Despite your fears, insecurities, and apprehensions, the world is waiting for you to show up on the other side.

CHAPTER 11

THERE MUST BE SOMETHING YOU NEED

Fuck it, I *will* paint.

I am ready. I will *live*. It's time for action! Yes, I will go *hard*.

I'm still willing to continue forward even though I can't see where the path is leading me. I got knocked down, but I am ready to climb. Although I do not fully comprehend my path, I am open to, and welcome, gaining understanding. I will continue to search for the light. People fail me all the time, but I will continue striving to love and understand them.

Against all odds I will continue being myself.

I will paint. I will paint. I will paint.

The instant you declare to *live life* and go hard, you are telling the Universe that you are ready to show up when life really starts to happen. Shitstorms may come your way—such as a flat tire, personal tragedy, or identity theft. Your washer and refrigerator may go out on the same day that your car's check engine light comes on. The check that you forgot you wrote six months ago finally gets cashed. The third-row seat of your Suburban may get stolen in the parking lot of Costco, right in front of a crowd of people eating at the food court. You might discover truths that you were previously blind to. You may begin to lose relationships with people who you thought would be in your life forever. Old childhood memories will come back and slap you in the face. Past relationships might play like a movie in the back of your mind. Shame and guilt will want their say. You may not get offered the job that you have been working towards. Your children may start to drive you crazy. A disconnect between you and your significant other may show its face in the form of frequent disagreements. Confidants may appear to turn their backs on you. And you may lose some loved ones. *Fucking confusing, right?*

I mean come on, I have decided to show up, and now "this."

"Why?!"

The question "Why?" is often hard to answer because, more often than not, additional information is not available. The elusive answers often reveal themselves in the obstacles that we face along the journey. And in some instances, we must be ready to embrace new lessons that will birth the answers that we seek.

In order to learn we have to pay attention to how we move through life, and what we allow to move *us*.

We have to at least attempt to avoid repeating the same behaviors that cause unpleasant situations in our lives. The roadblocks that inevitably materialize along our journey's path should leave us wondering if we missed a few signs that indicated whether we were headed in the wrong direction. Life will have you challenging the expectation that alarms "should" sound to warn you before you make your missteps.

Alternatively, you will question whether you chose to ignore that buzzing sound in your ear—or if the buzzing even existed at all. There are many factors at play that dictate whether we comprehend the lesson at hand.

We may not understand the situation the first, second, or third time around.

I have endured many circumstances where I simply did not grasp the situation/lesson that was on the table. I have attempted many times to give or *become* more, yet still ended up in the same predicament. The conclusion that I derived from that was:

Life will show up and continue to challenge you in many different areas, until you are ready to relinquish your ego in order to gain insight.

I am unsure about you, but I deal with these types of situations all the time.

A different kind of "butterfly effect." I was at a baseball game and saw a butterfly flapping its wings on the ground, seemingly unable to fly. I wanted to help, but could not gain access to the field due to the fact that the game was in progress. It was also quite a busy scene, since it was picture day for all the teams in the league. There were hundreds of kids and parents running around, tending to all of the activities taking place. I was in the zone for about an hour, just watching the butterfly flapping about slowly on the ground. I deduced that something must be wrong, if this flying insect was rendered flightless upon the ground. Yet I found that I was unable to locate it after looking away a couple of times.

To my surprise, it had gained momentum and mobility, and was eventually able to fly again. It was really a sight to see and I stood there in full amazement as if I had never seen a butterfly take flight. With my gaze fixed upon this butterfly, everything else around me came to a halt.

> ### *Though I desired to help it, I knew then that I would have been interfering with a struggle that needed to take place.*

Struggling is imperative to growth. Give a man a fish, and you feed him for a day; teach a man to fish and you feed him for a lifetime. If someone else is always helping us flap our wings, we will never learn to fly on our own. Watching the struggle and the triumph of that butterfly filled me with hope. Witnessing its empowered fragility opened my heart, and spoke loudly to my spirit. I heard: *Though you were designed to fly, it is okay that you are on the ground right now.*

That butterfly may have known what it was doing all along. I witnessed it as a struggle. Conversely, it could have been drying its wings, and laying low to ensure that it did not attempt to take flight prematurely, with wet, heavy wings.

There are many things that can render us flightless in life. A broken heart has surely drenched my wings; as well as loss, confusion, misunderstanding, not feeling heard, not feeling seen, just to name a few.

I can only hope that at the end of the day we are all striving to be a better version of ourselves.

No one wishes to feel and deal with the pain that rears its ugly head on the road to bettering ourselves, but there is no growth if we choose to reject the ugly truth of our present or past. We inflict more damage when we attempt to fly with damp, heavy wings.

Just as that butterfly did the work to flap its damp, heavy wings until they were dry enough to take flight, we must work through life's heaviness to spiritually ascend. We must accept and conquer life's challenges in order to grow. Then, and only then, do we allow ourselves the time to build up the knowledge and experience necessary to develop the strength for self-actualization and discipline.

If something is meant to fly, it will inevitably happen. Just as the caterpillar works and evolves through the stages of its lifecycle to culminate as a butterfly, we must work through each life lesson to bring us to enlightenment. You cannot skip steps in an attempt to rush the process. Skipping steps only ensures that the lesson will repeat itself, and re-emerge in your life until you learn from your mistakes. There is no "good" or "bad."

We have to accept that our thoughts, choices, and actions will always lead us somewhere.

We are always right where we need to be; meaning—right where our decisions have led us. Remember that you were designed to fly. And if life just so happens to have you on the ground, have faith in the fact that there must be something you need. Find out exactly what that something is and lean into it. And once you lean in, you will start to build the momentum you need to flap your wings.

When you are on the ground and
life feels like a ton of bricks on top of you,
hold on to my words:

THERE MUST BE
SOMETHING YOU NEED.

"IF YOU HAVE WINGS AND YOU'RE UNABLE TO FLY, THERE MUST BE SOMETHING ON THE GROUND THAT YOU NEED."

— SICOLA ELLIOTT

CHAPTER 12

BROKEN GLASS

Sometimes I just want to collect all the stressors present in my life, place them into a glass jar, seal it tight, then drop that little emotional bomb onto the floor—watching as the glass shatters every which way. The jar of choice must be glass to ensure that all the shit I put in it is visible before I throw it with all my might—and shatter the crap out of it.

Off the top of my head, there are a few things I can think of to place in that jar: reoccurring hurts from my past, disappointments, distractions, Facebook, e-mails, the attitudes of co-workers, all of the text messages from people asking for shit that they would never have the nerve to request if we were face-to-face. Of course, there's also: people's opinions, terrible drivers, and pretty much anything else that frustrates me. Oh, and let me not forget the people who don't cover their nose or mouth when they cough or sneeze; those people *definitely* make it into the jar!

I know, you're probably thinking, "Didn't you just dry your wings so that you can take flight?" ...and the answer is yes, but I can't fly carrying a whole bunch of bullshit around, now can I?

So just follow me here. Now that my imaginary jar is full of all the things that rub me the wrong way, I hold it tightly and—with all my might—I slam it down. I want glass flying *everywhere*, exploding like a wave crashing against a rocky shore! I want to be standing in the middle of the floor surrounded by shards of shattered glass. And after each piece finds its resting place around me, I want to grab a bat and really go to work, making sure that I beat the hell out of everything that's getting under my skin. After I complete that task, I will then grab a broom, a dust pan, and clean up and discard my mess.

Surprisingly, or perhaps not surprisingly, this fantasy does not stray too far from an incident that occurred between me and my husband.

The story plays out as follows:

It was a Saturday afternoon and
we were at home.

I was in the kitchen, minding my own business,
and attending to my own business.

From time to time—who am I kidding—most of the time, my husband and I argue over the dumbest things. I am almost positive it's not me, but rather has everything to do with him—and the blurry lens through which he sees life. The fact remains, we *argue*. We have the kind of arguments like, if I say the sky is blue, he'll look at that same sky and probably say, "Looks like we're going to get rain."

Crazy right? I mean a blue sky is just that—a blue sky. Well, not in my house. We argue over Christmas lights, or who turned off the sprinklers because the grass is now dying, or one of us just *assumes* the other has an attitude, and before you know it, we birth an argument. Since we are always getting into it about something dumb, I cannot recall what, exactly, sent me into a fury this particular Saturday afternoon.

If I let my husband add a line here
he would probably say that I am always in
a fury. So not true; you have to remember
that his life lens is a little blurry.

Anyway, I was washing dishes. He did, or was going to do, *something*, and I was pissed off. To let him know how irritated and mad I was, I allowed my dishwashing to grow louder and louder. I also ensured that every door got slammed shut after placing each dish into its respective cabinet.

"Bam! Bam! Bam!" was the soundtrack that came bellowing from the kitchen.

As for the spoons and forks, after washing them I would gather a bunch and drop them all at once—just to add a couple of tones to my soundtrack. I was wiping the countertops like a mad woman, moving about like I was racing for a prize. The last dish to be put away was a giant frying pan. Yes, a giant frying pan. *I already know what you're thinking; and, at the time, just maybe I was thinking the same thing.* At any rate, the frying pan lived in a bottom cabinet, just beside the stove. In my anger and frustration, I tossed the pan into the cabinet; and it had the nerve to fall out and crash onto the hardwood floor.

Any other day, in a more stable mood, I would have been more mindful of what I was doing. This pan is so large that there is a particular way that it needs to be stored in order to fit properly. But I was not in a "take your time" kind of mood. So, I picked up the pot again and, once more, tossed it forcedly into the cabinet.

> *It fell out and onto the floor,*
> *as if my husband had placed a minion*
> *in the cabinet to push that shit out,*
> *just to drive me crazy.*

By this time, I was enraged, because my acting out was turning into a bloopers reel. When you are pissed, the cabinet needs to slam continuously, and this giant frying pan was messing all that up.

Once more, I picked up the pan. But THIS time, I gripped the handle with my right hand and swung it like a tennis racket so that I could hit the other pot that was blocking it from getting into the cabinet. Perfect plan, because I was on a mission to make as much noise as possible.

However, I ended up hitting the corner of the stove's glass face.

Boom! It shattered into a million pieces, as if someone had taken a shotgun to it. And there I was, standing in the middle of it all, with no shoes to protect my bare feet.

Everyone came rushing in—because it truly sounded like someone had set off a bomb in the house. My husband rushed into the kitchen, and looked at me as if I were crazy. And, just to stay in character, I simply stared back at him and said, "The TV is next!" It was truly an accident, but he would never have believed it. Therefore, I had to wear the crazy hat just a bit longer.

After that, in a very calm voice, I asked one of my children to bring me my shoes and a broom.

As crazy as this may sound I was content with the mess that I had created, because it gave me an opportunity to see myself. It showed me how much power I had given away, to engage in the situation like I did.

It showed me how I actually still *reacted*, while at the time my life's focus was to learn how to *respond*. Though this situation was an accident, it never would have happened if I had not chosen to be reactive. It ended up costing me $275.00 and an ugly kitchen for a few weeks. (But if my husband ever asks, it was covered under the warranty. Wink-wink.)

The hypothetical shattering of a glass jar of emotions followed by my kitchen brawl story are indeed connected, and right in the middle of writing this chapter, I ironically had another incident that has something to do with shattered glass. (Yet again, surprising, I know.)

I am a mother of three children, two of which are teenagers and one that is 11 years old. My teenagers just turned thirteen and fourteen a day apart this month, which is October, so the puberty and everything that comes with it is alive, well, and popping off in my house—as are their mouths.

Lately, I have been around the house fussing a lot because no one wants to do what they are told to do. Not only that, but they spend more time auditing what the others did or didn't do. They have been complaining that *punishment* is not universal, and that they get into trouble for things the others don't. I wish like hell I could just refer them to a complaint department (a.k.a. a family therapist) to help them get their issues resolved.

I'm a barker, and with that being said...

...They never feel my bite.

In many ways I hate social media. I can't stand what it is doing to a whole generation of people. The biggest reason is that my kids think I pay for walking internet. They have made it their job to look at a phone 24/7, and since we have been dealing with so much this month with the kids—I was at a breaking point. I had had ENOUGH!

I was so sick of just barking. When I bark I say things like, "I'm going to crack that phone." "I am going to take that Xbox and throw it in the middle of the street!" "I'm cutting off the internet," or "I'm going to rip that TV off the wall!"

I'm well aware that I paid for all of those things, but the grief that these things are costing me in mental space? I'm discovering that they were not good investments. But I bark, I never bite. I'm like a broken record.

One day I finally reached my limit. I took a phone away and threw it at the wall—the strategy being that the screen would crack and make YouTube less attractive to watch. I was well aware of what I was doing. It was intentional and one hundred percent *not* out of rage.

What I did not anticipate happening was that I would pull the wrong phone out of the wrong pocket, and end up cracking my own screen. Funny, not funny—because now I am the one cutting my fingers on the screen. We're doubling down on the blooper reel, here.

Dramatic affect gone. Now I'm the crazy parent who can't even throw the right phone at the wall. I'm sure that is a story my kids will always tell.

But the real takeaway is this: Whether fantastical or literal, *shattering something* allowed me, yet again, the opportunity to examine what was "at hand"—"piece by piece."

When the kitchen scenario happened, I was at peace while cleaning up all the glass because, in that moment, something clicked. It was a *very long* moment, because glass had flown everywhere, and it took me some time to ensure "feet safety." But as I picked up the glass, a thought came to mind:

Take life piece by piece.
It's more effective to examine each
part rather than digest it whole.

There were many lessons that came out of the phone situation. One, parenting is hard as fuck. The fact that I had to attempt to prove myself with my outrageous act and outburst meant that communication was suffering. It meant that there was a breakdown somewhere on our communication assembly line. When you "communicate," you don't bark your orders, you explain what you are asking and what you expect and why it's important to you.

The biggest struggle with being great,
and I am great, is being consistent—even
when I am tested the most.

All my tests and hard lessons don't come from strangers, they come from the people that I live for and would die for. This made me realize that time is precious and I want to spend my time watering the seeds that I have planted in the hearts of my children, even when they make it hard, or are driving me insane. My job is to make sure that my love is the only thing that I am barking.

I tell you this story because I want to show you that, even in all my wonderfulness, I am human and I am still growing and working on myself every single day. I'm grateful that life continues to give me an opportunity to get it right. Attempting to conquer life one lesson at a time breeds progress, not perfection, and I'm okay with that.

Both situations gave me the opportunity to step back and take a breather. I realized that working towards the resolution had everything to do with my willingness to see myself. At the conclusion of each story, I was left with shattered glass that I would have to eventually clean up myself, items I'd have to replace, or—in the case of my phone—pay for a repair.

By doing so, I was able to reposition my perspective and recalibrate my emotional triggers and responses.

And what I told myself was, "Fuck it. Drop everything and start over. No big deal."

The very day I shattered my phone was the very day we had a serious family discussion. I'm sure my children all wanted to laugh about how poorly I pulled off my little stunt. But my husband, who wasn't surprised by my actions, said nothing. When I dig deep, I have to say that's a bit sad. I don't want the people closest to me accepting that I act a fool from time to time. I don't want my outbursts to become their norm when they think of me. It's pretty obvious that it's my husband's norm. That poor guy.

The phone incident made me think of a time when I was pregnant and my husband and I were at odds while driving. My husband was driving my car and at the time I had a radio where the face of the radio detached. I was pissed, so I wanted the music loud, and he decided to keep turning the music off. We battled back and forth until I took it upon myself to detach the radio, roll down the window, and I'm sure you know what came next.

Yes, I tossed that shit like it was nothing.

Circling back to now, I realize that my husband had no reaction then, either, because he was in no way surprised. He said "Sicola, you are volatile."

Eyes wide, chest out, I responded, "You've got to be kidding me!"

It would have rolled off his tongue and into my ears a little smoother if he had said, "Cupcake, sometimes you are unpredictable." But "volatile"? The definition of volatile is everything I'm *not* trying to be. I took it as an insult. My first thought was, "Shit, if he's the only person who sees this in me, then it must be him who brings out the worst in me."

Sounds about right, right? I'll answer that: Hell no, it doesn't sound right, and I realized that I needed to make some adjustments. So, I made a sign and posted it next to my bed with the word "volatile" on it, along with every synonym in the book.

People outside my home life think I'm great. Okay, I'm playing small here; they think I'm extraordinary, and that's cool, because I am. My passion, creativity, love for people, caring nature, and drive run a narrative through my life.

But my desire is that this narrative run through all of the environments and situations where my wonderful buttons are exposed. Situations where Little Sicola's fear, insecurities, lack of control, and self-worth issues are triggered. Those are the environments and situations that I desire to thrive in. Being "volatile" is not in alignment with that.

Our families and the people closest to us have access to our buttons, because they have full access to our past, and our habits. They get to see us in a light that most people will never see. Which means they also have the opportunity to push up against our buttons.

The person I am striving to be and working so hard to become does not want to be described as "unstable, uneasy, or explosive."

Knowing what I want and what I am striving for pushes me to look at the shattered glass from all angles. Those situations gave me the opportunity to look at myself and the role that I played in each predicament.

Now before you start dinging me for bad behavior, let me

reiterate—the glass jar is imaginary, and the whole kitchen scene was an accident. And the phone gaffe...well...lessons learned.

And what have I learned? I have learned that I'm okay with shattered pieces from time to time. If my gain is a new perspective, then it's worth the hassle of the clean-up. Sometimes you just have to take life in bite-sized pieces (of glass; perhaps a poor analogy here...) so you can examine them thoroughly. When things shatter there are pieces everywhere and it takes a great amount of courage to sit with yourself to figure out what pieces serve you, how they serve you, and what pieces do not.

Creating a scene in the kitchen because I was mad did not serve me. While cleaning up my mess, I discovered that. The phone situation opened my eyes to the area in my development that needed more attention.

I have an imaginary jar right now full of everything I do not want to be, while being fully aware of how some of those descriptions have played out in my life. My little notes read: *I am not unstable, I am not uneasy. I am not explosive, I am not eruptive, and I am for damn sure not volatile.* My hands are gripping each side of this imaginary jar—and on purpose and with purpose I drop this jar that is filled with everything I am not.

I have no intention of piecing any of this back together.

Going in, I am well aware that these characteristics do not serve me.

I will, however, sweep each piece into a dust pan and throw it the fuck away.

"Fuck it, drop everything" means that you drop things that do not serve your life in any way. Always seek out and take the lesson at hand, but do not hold onto things or allow things, people, or circumstances to occupy much-needed mental space. No excuses. The glass jar represents awareness, and if you look closely, you may see your image reflected back to you.

I told a friend the story about the cell phone fiasco and her response to me was, "Oh no, what did you learn?" I wanted to respond with, "Do you mean, what did my kids learn?" But I didn't because situations will always reflect back to us what we put out into the world.

I learned that I want my actions and behavior to represent the kind of person I desire to be. I'm learning each day to keep the things, people, and circumstances that serve me close. I learned that if I acknowledge the things, people, or circumstances that drive me crazy, I'm closer to finding new ways to deal with the annoyance.

For me the imaginary jar is just a tool I use to have a visual of somewhere to place my thoughts. In doing so, I am actively engaging and aware of my thoughts, aware of other people, and aware of situations that do not serve me. There are going to be times in life where you are going to have to say, "Fuck it, I'm dropping everything!" and there goes the glass jar—pieces shattered everywhere. Then after you do so, you either continue with the same old thoughts, people, things, or circumstances, or you sweep that shit up, dump it, and start over.

In the meantime, it wouldn't hurt to check out the extended warranty on your breakables.

"I MAY NOT KNOW
WHERE ALL
THE PIECES GO,
BUT PUT THE
PIECES IN MY
HAND AND I'LL
FIGURE IT OUT."

— SICOLA ELLIOTT

CHAPTER 13

I WILL SALT MY OWN FRIES

Stepping back to examine your life takes a great amount of courage. It also takes a lot of time and energy. As you may have noticed, I have evolved into a person who enjoys reflecting over her life. In doing so, I open myself up to discover new worlds within myself. I say "new worlds" because the discoveries are huge most of the time. But even if they are small, I treat them as if they are the missing piece to my life's puzzle. Often, I have found that some of these supposedly small discoveries scare the hell out of me.

Some are blissful awakenings, which require nothing more than experiencing enlightenment. Alternatively, some moments of enlightenment may ask that I adjust my attitude in order to live life harmoniously. I have learned that there is a time to be vocal, and a time to remain silent; that there is a time to be the teacher, and when we must be the student.

I am mostly the student.

As a matter of fact, I have enrolled as a lifetime member of the Learners' Club. Sure, there are some things that I can teach, but by being a student of life I'm often pushed to venture into the unknown; but what is added onto me because of those adventures is priceless. I have to put myself in a position where I am *conscious*—because I have had many unconscious moments, unknowingly giving my power away to someone or a situation to decide an outcome for me.

My unconscious behavior/default setting drives me to the mall or burger stands, and right past the gym, fully clothed in workout attire.

When this behavior is in the driver's seat I have a hard time maintaining a firm grip over my emotions, urges, responses, and—ultimately—my life. This happens to the best of us. One week we will be doing good on our goals and the next week we have a handful of M&M's with another bag stashed in our pockets.

I was standing in Wing Stop waiting on my food the day I realized that my default setting was calling the shots in my life.

I ordered the 10-piece Louisiana dry-rub chicken wings, which came with fries and a Coke. Oh, and a side of dipping Ranch! I called in my order so that it would be ready upon arrival—which it was not. So, in the meantime, I stood directly in front of the register to observe the employees that were preparing my food. *Observe* is a positive connotation for me staring them down as they worked. I people-watch all the time; especially when someone is handling my food. I shouldn't do this because people habitually touch their hair or wipe sweat from their brows. Oh God, and if I am in a restroom and an employee comes in and goes in the stall with their apron on, I will leave the restaurant before we get seated.

At home, I pray over my food to express gratitude. When eating out, one hundred percent of that prayer is out of hope that the people handling my food are adhering to sanitary food-handling protocols.

I am praying for the ones that touch their hair, or their face, or wipe sweat from their forehead. *I'm just praying over those hands.* So, with that being said, if I am allotted the chance to observe, I am obligated to watch and see what they do.

From my observation on this day, there were three employees working that shift. There was one on the register, one on the fryer, and one cleaning. I was watching the one who was cleaning, thinking to myself, "He better not try to help out with the food."

At this point, I'm all in: It's now imperative that I continue to watch what is going on behind the counter at this Wing Stop. (I don't even know how I eat out! Oh, never mind; I know the answer—it's pure laziness.)

With all these thoughts going through my mind, it became uncomfortably obvious that the amount of time I was spending standing at the counter could have been more wisely used at home, safely preparing my own meal. But my **default setting** had me convinced that eating out was the easiest way to satisfy my hunger.

The employee in the back was doing his thing. While tending to the chicken wings, he began to heavily salt a batch of fries just exiting the deep fryer. I thought, "Who the hell ordered extra salt?" He put so much salt on those fries that it prompted me to tell the employee behind the register to let the other guy know that I only wanted my fries *lightly salted*.

Once I was aware of Heavy Salt Tommy, I watched him like a hawk to make sure that he did what I requested of him.

I saw my order coming up and watched him, once again, pour a generous amount of salt onto the fries. MY fries. I mean, come on—where are the Salt Police when you need them?! I reminded the employee on the register that I wanted my fries lightly salted, alerting her that her heavy-handed co-worker had put too much salt on my fries. She said, "No problem," and went on to whisper something into his ear.

I expected to wait a bit longer for my food, considering the fact that he was going to have to make me a new batch of fries with less salt.

I was laser-focused on him, and every move that he made.

What he did next almost made me jump over the counter and slap the fries out of his hand.

He took the heavily-salted fries out of the bag and, instead of throwing them out, *threw them back into the oil*—in an attempt to serve them to me again. I guess he thought that frying them a second time would rid them of the extra salt. I allowed the employees to go through the motions of bagging my food once more, but as the girl was getting ready to hand my food to me, I leaned in and whispered,

"If you don't get those fries out of my bag..."

Then I raised my voice—just a little bit—and said, "I said light salt on my fries! You guys messed up, and to correct the problem you double-dip my fries in oil?! The food is already fried. What made you think that I want to eat extra oil? Did I order extra oil?!"

I was hot.

The girl responded with, "No problem. More fries are coming out, and I will make sure that they are right." They gave me a new batch of fries. But I stormed out of there pissed, thinking of all the shit I was going to tell the corporate office when I got with them!

While driving away I thought to myself, "What the fuck is going on here, and why am I really mad?"

The answer to that question is very simple:

You cannot give someone your power,
and then grow angry when they do what they
please with their newfound empowerment.

I gave Heavy Salt Tommy the power to put whatever amount of salt on my fries that he saw fit. I let him decide the amount of times he was going to shake that damn salt shaker over my deep-fried potatoes. So, I had to ask myself, "Who are you really mad at?"

And in that moment, I decided that I wanted to salt my own damn fries. I wanted to hold the salt shaker and shake it over my life. You see, I really couldn't be mad at anyone.

Honestly, I am sure that I was attempting to eat healthy at that time and had no business even pulling into the parking lot of Wing Stop. The heavy-handed employee was just doing his job. And maybe that's just how he likes his fries. I gave up my power when I called in that order, knowing that my house and kitchen were less than half a mile away.

On my three-minute ride home, something clicked for me and my eyes were wide open to what I had given up. There was no turning back; I was fully aware.

So, I have to ask, to what or to whom are you giving your power?

Who is holding the saltshaker in your life?

Remaining silent is compliance, which is just as powerful as giving verbal permission. There are so many roles to play in life. Will you be the lead in yours? When you prepare your canvas and paint your own portrait, make sure it shows you salting your own damn fries.

I know I will be salting mine.

This page was left blank for you...fill it with your thoughts.

CHAPTER 14

F*CK PERFECTION

According to Webster's New Collegiate Dictionary (1979), "Experiment" is defined as "an operation carried out under controlled conditions in order to discover an unknown effect or law, to test or establish a hypothesis, or to illustrate a known law." (p. 399)

For me, the "hypothesis" represents life, and the "experiment" is how I choose to live it.

Perfection is not expected during the scientific process, nor is it feasible during the trials and errors of life. We are here to continuously make new discoveries, and part of that means that we will continuously make mistakes. Making mistakes, and having wrenches thrown into our plans left and right, is a means by which we evolve and change. Life will lend us many opportunities to start again, which means *circumstances* are nothing more than new opportunities for further investigation. Life can get scary sometimes because we enter into new experiences with limited knowledge, and have no idea how things will turn out.

I remodeled my bathrooms a couple of years ago, and I remember being on edge when it came time for them to begin tearing down the walls. We were excited to get started, but when the contractor told us on a Friday evening that he could start the following Monday, I was overcome with uncertainty.

My excitement suddenly turned into a bucket of "what ifs."

My mind was plagued with thoughts of all that could go wrong. I was thinking about my budget, and how I did not want to exceed it. I wondered, "What if something is behind the walls?" Then that seed of fear really gained traction in my head: "If something is behind these walls, wouldn't I want to know about it? Wouldn't I want to fix it?" At the time, the answer was both "yes" and "no." Yes, I would want to know. Simultaneously, I did not want to know, rationalizing that it would be a good time to take on my husband's attitude—"Why fix what isn't broken?"

My fear of the unknown was speaking for me, as well as influencing my actions. I guess it is safe to say that I wanted everything to be *perfect.* But perfection is heavy. The stress and worry are just not worth it.

There is nothing perfect about tearing down walls. It is just a mess. And it's the same with life, when we have to tear down emotional walls that we have built up. We have to be willing to deal with the hidden messes of life, and we can't accomplish that by expecting everything to be perfect.

With all that said, I have to be honest: I was a nervous wreck throughout the demolition process.

> *If you thought Heavy Salt Tommy had it bad, I damn near was riding on the backs of the contractors, trying to make sure nothing went wrong!*

(As if I could fix it, if it did.)

Ultimately, all went well, I was relieved—and the contractors more than likely could relax, safe in the knowledge that they no longer had to consider the need to file a restraining order against me. The unknown did not kill me, or break my bank account. **The unknown was the experiment.** I told myself that it is perfectly acceptable to be a bit fearful of what you might discover or uncover, but not being willing to investigate the situation was unacceptable.

*In order to grow past my fear,
I had to experiment. It was scary and
exciting at the same time.*

I was beyond nervous to tear down the first wall in the first bathroom, but by the time we got to the second bathroom I was at ease. And it's good that I was, because when we tore down the walls in that second bathroom, we discovered that the (presumably) original builders had put up drywall right over stucco! But since my mind wasn't wrapped around perfection anymore, I was able to handle the situation at hand with a level head. And by the time we reached the third bathroom, I was like, "Give me the hammer, because I am ready!"

Life is the hypothesis, how we live it and handle things is the experiment. Overcoming my fear and working through the obstacles is what prepared me to take hammer in hand, and feel the confidence to take a swing at tearing those walls down. I was more knowledgeable and therefore eager to find and fix a problem, if there was one present.

*That's how we need to approach life; with a
"fuck it" attitude and a hammer.*

We have to tear some shit down if we want to get away from living a superficial life of lies. The days of looking good on the outside while being plagued by hidden rot underneath our drywall are over. Experiments exist because there are no quick fixes or answers to big situations or questions. You have to get down and dirty with life. You have to fail, and fail again. Failure is the only vehicle that spurs you to develop the skills necessary to elevate yourself into new levels of understanding. If everything were easy you would never grow; simply because you would not have a reason to push yourself towards something greater.

Are the experiments of life often frightening? Yes; *but aren't they also exciting*? I like to think of myself as a detective. I look for clues, formulate questions that guide me to seek answers, and then I accept each new discovery because it brings forth new knowledge and insight.

The tools that are required and necessary to overcome obstacles are often found in the obstacle itself. I can't solve the problem in the wall unless I tear down the wall. It turns out that strength can be found while sorting through broken pieces. We must remain open in order to tackle life's obstacles, and work through the shit that life brings. I'm sure you have seen the signs that read, "Work in Progress." That means that something is going on. Oftentimes the "work in progress" areas are restricted, and for good reason. Shit can get messy; and it's the same when you are working your way through life.

I have never seen a sign that reads, "Perfection in Progress," and if I did I would probably tear it down.

During the experiment we have to be open and ready to receive and take in whatever comes our way. We have to pay close attention to what is going on in order to note what worked, what didn't, and what our takeaways will be. After doing so we have to figure out how the takeaways can serve us in our life.

Perfection is the devil. Holding onto the idea that you are perfect or that things need to be perfect, keeps you from ascending. Conversely, attempting to reach perfection will stop you before you ever begin. Reaching for perfection is not feasible; and besides, it takes up way too much energy. To be perfect means you are free of flaws, and I don't know about you, but my flaws tell one hell of a story. I can't speak about growth without acknowledging my flaws.

We can't be so afraid of messing up that we don't allow ourselves to live. At the beginning of last year, my friend and I decided that we would hold each other accountable in reaching our goals or practicing our craft. I shared with my friend that I wanted to be a motivational speaker/life coach, and I needed to find out if I had what it takes to motivate people. I decided that I would record a one-minute video each day just for practice.

Blooper here, blooper there, blooper everywhere.

But it was practice, so I sent them anyway. I came across those same videos almost a year later and the craziest, most outrageous thought came to mind: *I should post these.*

I thought to myself, "Hell no," followed by my next thought of, "Why not?" That "why not" thought is all about the experiment. I had nothing to lose. I like to say that perfection is not my aim, so just to prove it to myself and challenge myself, I posted three videos to two social media outlets. Talk about letting myself be seen!

And guess what? I am still standing. Still in one piece. But now, I'm even *more* eager to let myself be seen and work through the experiment.

So, fuck perfection, because there is none to be found in the tests and trials of life. And if people don't like what your tests and trials look like, let *them* deal with that.

Just be sure that you keep showing up for yourself.

This page was left blank for you...fill it with your thoughts.

CHAPTER 15

WHO DOES SHE THINK SHE IS?

Do we need to bring our own jam? I joined Toastmasters in January of 2018. If you're thinking, "What the heck is Toastmasters?" you're not alone, because I was thinking the same thing when I first heard of it. I follow Mel Robbins and was watching a YouTube video where a woman asked the million-dollar question: something like, "I want to do what you do. Where can I start to embark on this motivational speaking journey?"

Good question, right? That question was probably on the mind of everyone in the room. But the good thing about being in a room with a crowd hungry for knowledge is it's likely that someone else will have the courage to ask the question that is on everyone else's mind. And when that one person opens their mouth, all heads are down—taking notes on the answer.

Had that been me, and Mel Robbins were Oprah, my question would have been, "How can I be you?" I'm sure Oprah would say something like, "Honey, you were born to be *you* and bring *your* gifts to the world!"

I would have laughed it off—just to act like I was kidding—then hit her with, "Well, how can I be a version of what you've got going on?"

> **It's Oprah, people: I have to go
> hard or go home.**

But in this particular Mel Robbins YouTube episode, Mel answered the question by telling the woman that she should join Toastmasters and, being the student that I am, I took it straight to Siri to see what I could find out.

"Siri, what is Toastmasters?"

"*Toastmasters is a club to hone public speaking and communication skills.*"

"Siri, where can I find a club?"

Boom, done! There was a club 3.2 miles from my house at the Marriott Hotel that met on Friday afternoons.

> **See how fast you can go from knowing
> nothing about anything to knowing a little
> bit about something?**

First meeting that I attended, I volunteered to do an ice breaker question. This is an impromptu question that you have to answer on the spot, and you're only allotted two minutes to do it. I wasn't there to play any games, so I just threw myself out there. Mainly because I hate to be called on, but also because I was on a mission. I liked the group, and joined the club that day.

Once you become a member of Toastmasters, the first speech you have to give is your "five-minute ice breaker" speech to introduce yourself to all the club members. As I pondered on how I wanted to present, a title idea came to mind: "Who does she think she is?"

I thought this title was perfect for me, as I often get the feeling that this is a question that runs through people's minds before they get to know me.

> ***My personal "Who do I think I am" moments take a lot of courage and a whole lot of nerve for me to confront.***

I started off my speech by telling the group how I thought my title was original until I typed it into Google, only to discover a documentary entitled:

"Who Does She Think She Is? *'Who Does She Think She Is' is a documentary about five women striving to balance their artistic pursuits while raising children.*"

At first, I was like, "Damn! That was my title!" until I realized that this title holds great meaning for many women trying to pursue their dreams, overcome a variety of obstacles, or simply trying to find their voice. It was proof that this attitude/energy is not just something that I have, but something that lives in the hearts of many women who have the courage to act on it.

It takes guts to be *me* and carry myself in this way, and it's nice to know that my tribe is out there somewhere.

"Who does she think she is?" is more than an attitude. It's a chip on our shoulders that allows us to kick in doors we otherwise would have never had the courage to step in front of.

I was trying to gather my thoughts for this Toastmasters speech, recollecting moments when I have summoned this attitude to get something done, and realized that I carry this attitude with me more often than not.

My answer to the "who do you think you are" question is simple; I'm whoever I want to be.

Some might think that's cocky, but thinking of myself in this way has opened so many doors, changed so many minds, and at times even changed the game.

Here are some examples…

I Start at "No"

When I was in my twenties, I had done some damage to my credit. I received my first credit card right out of high school and felt like I had hit the lotto. It was a GTE Visa in the amount of five hundred dollars. Knowing absolutely nothing about credit, I thought that it was cool to just hang up on the people when they called and asked for their payment. Pure ignorance, I know.

And…what I *really* didn't know then was that negative marks would remain on my credit for seven years. But since I am the queen of making up my own rules, I took every collection account and worked the hell out of it. Meaning I negotiated like I was a credit pro and knew everything that had to do with credit. I wrote letters and contacted each credit card collection company. And these were basically "demand" letters because, for some reason, I thought that I was in a position to do so. I requested that they remove all negative items from my credit report and if they agreed to do so, then I would pay my debt.

> **The only thing that I could leverage in this situation was the fact that I refused to take "no" for an answer.**

It was a journey, but good thing for me the collection companies

174

that I dealt with were really small. They advised me many times that it was the law, and that they were unable to take things off my credit. Time after time they told me no. And since I had no interest in speaking to someone who carried the rule book in their back pocket, I would say, "No problem," hang up, then pick up the phone only to call right back hoping to reach the right person.

I didn't mind having to do that multiple times. I called in so much, they flagged my account so I would get transferred to the same mean ass representative every time. It was clear that they started to enjoy telling me no.

After wearing them down (and wearing on their nerves), I got exactly what I requested. I started getting letters that read, "In response to your inquiry, we requested that the consumer reporting agencies delete the delinquency(s) from your credit report."

That letter was dated June 7, 2006, and that was the date I discovered my power.

When you have a blank canvas, you are starting with nothing—and that's the beauty of it. I personally like to start at no. When someone tells me that I can't do something or something can't be done, I make it my duty to change that shit.

I pushed. I had the nerve to request things that I was in no position to request, but I one hundred percent believed in my desired results. My **belief** did all the heavy lifting and provided the energy that pushed me forward.

I just blossomed in the results.

State Your Purpose

I work for a school district. Once a year, they send out an email to solicit presenters for their event where teachers teach teachers. It's a full day of workshops where you learn from your peers. I am in no way a teacher; well, not a credentialed classroom teacher, and I am pretty sure that the teachers in this district wouldn't consider me their peer in the professional realm. But I opened that email and read through it anyway.

A thought crossed my mind right before I was getting ready to hit Delete: "I should apply." I knew the email was in no way addressed to me, and it just went out to the whole district. But when you believe in yourself, you also believe that you are able, and can do anything. Not having a teaching credential didn't make my voice less powerful in my opinion. So I opened that application, filled it out, and this Campus Supervisor hit "send."

I sent it with nothing attached.

Meaning, my "worthiness" was not attached to the outcome.

I did not have a "desired" outcome. All I had was my willingness to *show up*—and in that moment, that was all that mattered. I'm pretty sure when my application crossed the desk of the district head, they thought to themselves, "Who does she think she is?" And if they asked themselves that question, I'm sure they wanted to find out, because the next email read, "Congratulations, you have been chosen to be a presenter."

The title of my workshop was so different from the others. There were titles like, "Understanding the AP rubric from the perspective of an AP reader," or, "Dealing with documents—SBAC & Common Core application for every level," and the list goes on.

My title was simple: **"State Your Purpose."**

"State Your Purpose" was designed as a collaborative workshop where groups of four to five would work together to share ideas and combine all of those ideas to make one powerful statement. During planning, I had ten teachers sign up for my workshop, but on the day of the workshop I ended up with only three—a football coach, a drama teacher, and an English teacher.

Some might think: How embarrassing; out of nine hundred teachers you only had three show up? But for me it was the most amazing experience. You see, it had nothing to do with the teachers and everything to do with me. And I was so damn proud of myself for having the courage to even do it, I didn't care about the numbers. When you think highly of yourself, how can others NOT follow suit?

As I am writing this it gives me the chills because, as a young woman, I wouldn't even call McDonald's to ask if they were hiring. Oh, the things I would tell my younger self. I have gotten so much accomplished with this edge that I now carry around, because it keeps me challenging myself to prove to myself *who I think I am.*

My grandmother used to tell me all the time how persistent I was. And she would say it in a way where she had just given up, because I would not stop asking until her no became a yes.

"Coco, you are so persistent."

And even though my grandmother is gone, I still hear her voice, and I thank her—because now those words hit my ears as the best compliment.

It is now a "must" that I live up to it.

~~~

The Ellen Show

Late in 2017, I wrote to The Ellen Show. The question she had asked was related to her Million Acts of Kindness campaign, and I took it upon myself to write in about who I was. If you don't praise yourself, who will? What I wrote was short and sweet, and in my usual fashion, after I hit send, I didn't give it another thought.

January 2018 came around and I got a phone call from a number in Burbank. To my surprise, it was a producer with The

Ellen Show. I was in the kitchen, cleaning chicken at the time, and the voice on the phone said, "We were inspired by your story. Can you tell us more about yourself?"

With salmonella from the chicken I had been preparing all over my hands, I couldn't touch anything, and now I had to think on the spot. I kind of went straight into panic mode and thought to myself:

"Shit! I just joined Toastmasters and haven't practiced my elevator speech yet!"

I started pacing around the house, trying to think of the best spiel I could about who I was and how I could explain that in such a short period of time. I was lost for words, verbally stumbling all over myself, but made it through. She thanked me for my time, gave me a heads up on the date—if I were to get a call back—and said goodbye.

I got off the phone and wanted to melt, because I had forgotten to mention a lot of the things that I do in the community.

I had to stop myself before opening the gate to negative thoughts, and gave myself a moment to regroup.

I had to remind myself that I live a life full of blank canvases and carry an attitude of unlimited possibilities, and when I do that, I am able to paint whatever I like.

It didn't matter that I thought I did horribly on the phone. That was just one moment in time. My power lies in what I do with my next moments.

So, with my next moment, I went right into my office and locked that date in. I wrote on my calendar in bold lettering: **"You are going to the Ellen show."** I was not at all sure if the producer had chosen me, but I just knew that my mind was made up. And if my mind was made up how could she not choose me?

After collecting my thoughts, I went crazy searching for the email that had gotten me a phone call back from the show. I had written to the show then promptly forgot all about it. Hell, writing in and getting your letter read is like winning the lotto! I mean, come on, how great were the chances? I can only imagine how many people write the show each day, and for my letter to stand out—it must have been pretty amazing!

So I figured I'd better find out what I had written.

My online entry was short and sweet. I told them a little about myself, what I've done in the community, and what I desired to do. The ending of my entry is what I believe got me a phone call. This is how I ended my letter after I gave my spiel about who I was:

"Ellen, it's really hard to write about myself, but I'm extraordinary and although you don't know it yet, I invite you to find out."

Who in the hell invites *Ellen* to find out who *they* are? Most people are trying to just meet Ellen, and here I am letting Ellen know it's cool you're famous and all, but you need to meet me. I couldn't believe I had hit send on that one! Some nerve, right?

Who do I think I am? And if I felt like "Who do I think I am?" after reading what I wrote, I'm sure the producer had the same sentiment, and if that crossed her mind, I could only hope that she would want to find out.

Turns out she did.

I got a call back the next day with my official invitation to the show. And THIS show just so happened to be Ellen's 60th Birthday Party. Michelle Obama was there, for goodness sake. I was only like twenty feet away from Michelle—my mouth totally dropped and hanging there when she walked out!

I wanted to run on that stage so bad,
but I didn't think it was a good day to get
tackled and thrown in jail.

It was Ellen's birthday, but I felt like it was mine, and the surprises kept rolling in. Everyone in the audience was personally invited for their acts of kindness and the energy that filled that place was everything. With Ellen, you never know what you are going to get; you just know that you are going to get *something*.

And because of my courage and belief in myself, I got to split one million dollars with the audience.

I have to say that I was impressed with myself. But then realized that I have summoned this attitude and courage many times in my life. People may not say "who does she think she is" out loud, but I always make sure I don't leave people wondering.

~~~

WHO DO I THINK I AM?

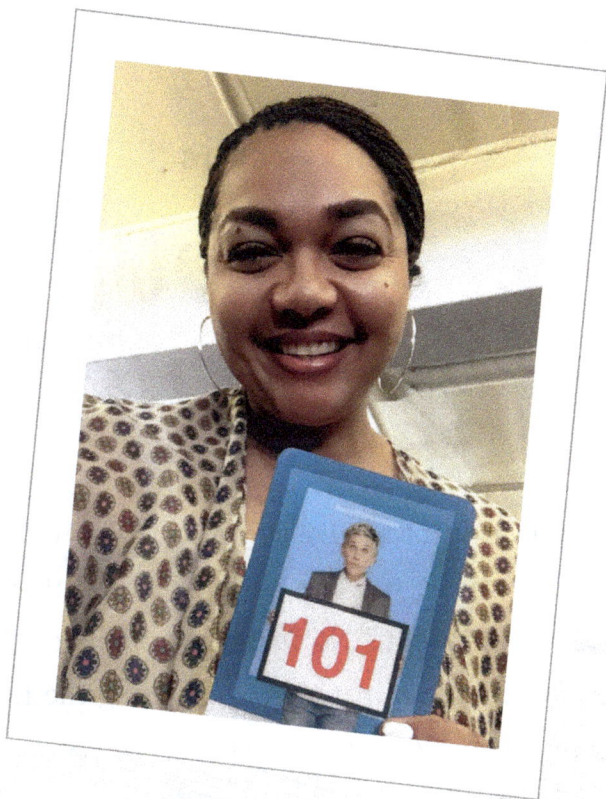

I THINK I'M A GIRL
WHO GOT MYSELF A SEAT
ON THE ELLEN SHOW.

CHAPTER 16

PLAY YOUR CARDS RIGHT

I f you ever want to give someone advice using as little as four words, you can simply just tell them to "play their cards right." No further explanation is needed, but most of the time instead of just using the four words, we add two more words to make it six, "*You better* play your cards right."

> *This statement implies that opportunity may be lurking in the hand that we were dealt.*

You card players out there know what I mean.

The deck gets shuffled. One by one, the cards slide over each other. I'm sure you enjoy the soundtrack that the shuffling provides; the whisper of wind produced by the flick of your finger, the sound growing louder as the cards are forced on top of one another—and then *Bam!*—the check hit of the deck to the table to get all the cards aligned.

The dealer is ready to deal.

Since the deck of life comes with any—and every—thing one could imagine, being on the receiving end we hope that we are dealt a good hand. In life's deck of cards lie the answers, the opportunities, and the obstacles. One card could benefit the next, while another card might weaken the hand all together. Those realties are just a part of life.

Growing up, a family get-together wasn't a get-together if a card game wasn't being played or about to be played. Bid Whist and Spades were the card games of choice, and today I am not sure how I made it through my childhood only knowing how to play Speed.

Life's deck of cards is full of mystery. We don't know what cards we will be dealt; we just hope the cards give us an advantage over the other players. You know, set us up for a win.

We only get a glimpse of one side until we flip them over.

When my brother Jared passed away, it made me want to play life like I played Speed. It made me want to win quick, be the fastest to organize my cards, lay them down in order, and be the first to slam my last card down and declare "speed." Some people may call that being ambitious, and I can see that, but something else was operating in me. It wasn't that I developed a competitive nature, or got a gust of motivation to go harder than I have ever gone before.

Conversely, I was operating in moments where the thought of life being short scared the hell out of me, which made me feel rushed to get things done. I was scared to waste any time. If something wasn't making me feel happy *instantly*, I panicked. The shadow of my brother's premature death had me thinking and knowing life was just way too short. And indeed, it is; but I was wasting *more* time thinking about the time I didn't want to waste.

And when I thought about it, I realized those thoughts were really counterproductive. In no way had I come this far to produce the opposite of what I desired.

Then I thought of the joker card. The joker card is the wild card and, in my family, if you have that joker card in your hand you feel empowered instantly, knowing at any time you can bend the game towards your advantage. That one card has the power to shift the direction of things. All rules go out the window when someone slams that joker card down and lets their demands be known.

*I now truly understand that, by playing
my cards right in life, I no longer need the
joker card to be physically in my hand to know,
or understand, the power I possess to shift or
bend things to my advantage.*

Although fear seemed to be driving my thoughts, which brought on the panic, I was okay with it, because grieving is a process, and I was able to realize that something else was revving my life's engine. I had now reached a point where I self-checked and self-corrected all the time. When I'm grieving, I no longer attempt to downplay those feelings. Instead, I attempt to understand them as they arise. You could call this my own personal brand of "interpretation after the investigation."

Here was my inner dialogue:

"Something greater is going on within you. The uneasiness of time wants you to emerge differently in your life. It's coming up as fear and has you feeling anxious, but it's directing you toward your magic—so grab ahold of it and bend it, so you can point it in the right direction. Show up, speak up, show out. Some people take a number, I want you to walk right up to the window."

This was my inner dialogue at the time, but I'm now asking YOU to take it as a personal message from me to you, the reader.

"Show up, speak up, and show out" is the theme of my life's deck of cards. And each card I use is a display of my personal power threaded with the understanding of each cord I untangled.

I'm getting what I want out of life. Getting the results that I desire. Putting things in place for my next move, and not feeling forced to do any of it because, with growth, it comes naturally.

With all of this growth, it's a must that I show up; and if I show up, it's a must that I speak up, and if I speak up, then you know I've got to show out. *Hashtag* "my magic," *hashtag* "worth the journey."

I can't speak for anyone else, so I will use an "I" statement here, and "I" feel obligated to play my cards right and expose people to my light. In doing so, my teenage heart burns inside of me.

I push myself to always seek out my highest self so that I can have a positive impact on the hearts of teenage girls, as well as the teenage heart that is still crying out in each woman.

The biggest shipment of my life arrived at my door one day recently. It was the first pressing of the motivational deck of cards I had created for teenage girls. The order quantity was twenty-five hundred and, in my mind, I was thinking no big deal; I'll just stack them in my office. To my surprise and bad judgment, the *pallet* was huge. Yes, pallet. Not "package."

It was tall enough and wide enough for me and three other adults to sit on with our feet dangling. I looked at my husband like, "Oops. Looks like these are going in the garage." I was overwhelmed with excitement, and I still am, because these cards represent where my heart is, my message, and how creative I am.

But more importantly, they are an avenue for and opportunity to be the person I needed when I was a teenage girl.

I call them **My Teenage Heart Collection** because my vision for what this will be is vivid. I created the deck of cards to fill any voids or the absence of support in the lives of teenage girls, but more importantly I want to teach them how to develop their inner voice.

Since my life has a lot to do with self-motivation, I can't live this life without teaching teenage girls how it's done. My goal is to expand their confidence, renew their determination, and inspire them to start over in any situation.

Who knew that by playing my cards right, I would create motivational cards that teach young girls and women how to play theirs?

My products came before I had devised my plan, and I am just now learning how to sell things, but it's a whole new, wonderful journey.

At least I have enough cards.

Right now in my life I am getting what I want because I don't like being told no. And when you don't like being told no, you become resourceful. And when you become resourceful, it makes you want to go out on your OWN. You get it? OWN? (This time, it WAS "pun intended.")

I'm showing up for myself because I have read too many of Brené Brown's books not to put all that wisdom and insight into practice. I love this quote by Brené Brown: "Integrity is choosing courage over comfort. Choosing what is right over what is fun, fast or easy: and choosing to practice our values rather than simply professing them. Sounds like showing up to me." (Rising Strong, pg. 98.)

I'm speaking up because in most circumstances it's the right thing to do, and at other times, I just have something to say. Marianne Williamson captured my feelings perfectly when she wrote, "As we let our light shine, we unconsciously give other people permission to do the same."[2]

With growth I'm not just playing my hand, I have possession of the whole deck—and all the paint. And not because it comes easy, but more so because I'm willing to do the work.

---

[2]Williamson, Marianne. "Return to Love: Reflection on the Principles of 'A Course in Miracles.'" pp. 190-191.

When I think about putting in work for what you want out of life and playing your cards right, I think of my favorite movie of all time, "Men of Honor." Cuba Gooding Jr. plays Carl Brashear, the first African American master diver in the U.S Navy. Master Chief Billy Sunday, played by Robert De Niro, gives Brashear a really hard time. Carl Brashear was continuously being dealt a bad hand—a hand of cards that were intended to keep him down. In one of the scenes, Carl Brashear is in the library looking for a tutor so he can pass his exam to remain in the diving program that he was never supposed to be in.

The way I see it, he took the hand he was dealt, put those cards in his back pocket, and went out to seek another hand. And who said any of us have to keep the hands we were dealt? Take what you need from them, of course, the lessons or whatever you need to learn, but you don't have to keep them.

Who said those cards would be the cards that would define you?

Dysfunction and domestic violence were hands that I was dealt, but those cards no longer define me. They don't even define my parents anymore.

> ***Like Carl Brashear, in any situation I go looking for the hand that best fits where I desire to be. We have choices, people.***

Life moves or stops by the hand of our choices. It's just like I tell my children: Life is full of choices and you get to make one. Meaning, I can't make the choice for you. But back to Carl Brashear and the scene that made such an impact on me. In this scene, a woman in the library asks Carl, "Why do you want it so bad?" His response gives me chills. He turns to her and says, "Because they said I couldn't have it."

Carl Brashear's energy and focus represents everything we need to play our cards right in life. The way I see it his mental strength, will, and energy sent a memo to life that read:

> *"To Whomever It May Concern:*
>
> *I think you gave me the wrong cards to play in life. I looked at my hand, have lived my hand, have made some important discoveries, and have grown, but I need to return the cards that were dealt to me because it's obvious you had no idea who I planned on becoming.*
>
> *Sincerely,*
> *Carl Brashear"*

That's how I do it people. The memo above is how I move through life. I've got that Carl Brashear, "I'm coming for you," kind of energy. I'm not here to settle for less than I deserve. I'm not here to live my life through other people.

I am here to play my cards right and return the ones that no longer serve my life's purpose.

I'll start at "no" with no problem. I'll see opportunity where others see none. And I will stand in my integrity and enjoy the momentum fueled by my choices. When I play the game of life this way my energy sends out signals that I am unstoppable.

But I never leave home without a pocket full of advice that someone once gave me, that I want to share with you. It's only six words:

YOU BETTER PLAY YOUR CARDS RIGHT.

CONCLUSION

I t's 11:51 p.m. and I am sitting in my office, which is now located in our dining room. I guess it was time to give all the kids their own rooms, so I got the boot. Not sure where we got that idea—I never had my own room growing up.

So, while my kids are up in their rooms living their best lives, my office is located right next to the kitchen. To my left is a window and to my right...is the damn refrigerator and stove—with a new glass face.

I try not to look that way because who wants to think about cooking or know how many times the kids actually go in the refrigerator each day while trying to be creative? The tallies I have on them are insane, so now without even looking up I say, "Get out of there, you ate already!" (There are three of them, so I'm looking into training an "Alexa" to work off of motion sensor to shout it for me.) The kitchen is the one room in the house where, if it's dirty, it messes up the energy of the whole the house.

Is it just me?

You know how you start a job, and in the job description they list the working conditions? Well, if my office location came with one it would read as follows:

"Privacy: none. You are located in the dining room. Subject to hearing the washer and dryer at a volume which evokes a sense of working in the laundry room. Productivity will be regulated by children entering and taking inventory of cabinet and refrigerator contents throughout the work day. The proximity of your office to multiple corridors allows you to be available and accessible to any person with the last name 'Elliott.' Keeping the door ajar will allow the resident dog to bark every time another dog walks by. We recommend that you close the door before making business calls."

I may have to terminate this contract soon.

Right now, my door-less, wall-less office looks like a tornado paid me a visit because I have surrounded myself with every book that I have read, every note I have jotted down, and all my journals.

For the first time in the process of writing this book, I'm actually thinking about the book.

I know that sounds crazy but it's true. Let me try to explain. I'm a creative person and, for me, every detail of what I want to do does not need to be planned. After designing my motivational cards for teenage girls on my iPad with an app and my finger, I kept telling my husband that I needed to get my hands on the new iPad Pro and an Apple pen because, "When I do, I promise you—I am going to become an artist."

We went to the mall one day and I was looking a mess, so I really didn't want to walk around, but my husband said, "Come on..." and at the same time was looking at me like, "I know you're not trying to look cute for anybody in this mall, and I've been looking at you all day with this scarf on your head..."

We made our way to the Apple store and he asked me, "Which one do you want?" Oh, I got one! But once home, the kids looked at my husband like, "How dare you buy her one. We are all due for an upgrade!" BRATS. I busted that iPad out right in front of my three crumb snatchers, and I have been drawing ever since. When I draw I don't have a plan, or any idea of what I want my drawing to look like. I'm not attached to the outcome in any way, shape, or form. I'm just drawing, no thinking involved, just letting the pen flow.

The feedback I have been getting is crazy. People inbox me and ask if I can draw them specific things. My reply is, "I can't draw like that." I posted a dreamcatcher that I had drawn, and my friend commented on my post and said, "I wish I would have had you draw my dreamcatcher for my tattoo." I replied and told her, "When you got that tattoo, I didn't know that I could draw a dreamcatcher."

My point is this:

I don't know what I have in me until I put the pen to the paper, or the paintbrush to the canvas.

Way back when, I simply said I wanted to write a book. I didn't plan it out, and had no idea how it would turn out. My choice just kicked into action.

But now I'm over here *thinking*...and with my flow, that's a recipe for disaster. That's an invitation for writer's block. And when I experience writer's block I can still *write*—but when I'm done, none of it makes sense. If I'm writing too much, then I'm thinking too much, and if I'm thinking too much, what I produce is not authentic. And if it's not authentic, then count me out.

I have to draw on my mental strength here and find my footing, because my inner voice has questions: "How do I end this book? Do I drop the paintbrushes that are dripping with paint? Do I gently lay them down? Do I place them in someone else's hands?"

Do I throw them? Rinse them? What am I going to do with them?

And after a few moments of silence a little voice in my head said, "Do all that shit."

This is how I paint.

I live in the same house. It's yellow with white trim. I drive the same car; it's a desert sand color (brown). I have the same husband, he's surviving Sicola. I would say that I have the same children, but with them I don't know which mood will show up as their representative at any given moment, so each day is an adventure.

I am sitting in the same room where I made the life-altering decision to close my childcare business. It's a room where I've changed diapers, wiped noses, and got coughed on a million times. The walls in here were once yellow to keep the kids in a upbeat mood. And as I sit here with that memory, all I can do is smile. I made a hard decision for myself and it's working out.

But I know you must be wondering what has changed.

The answer to THAT question is easy: all the little things.

When I pick up a paintbrush (...or iPad Pro...) and begin to paint, I find myself more interested in the flow than I am in any lines. More interested in the blend than I am in the structure. And *way* more interested in the motion of the colors than I am in the outcome!

"Flow" is steady and continuous movement, and no one but you can determine your pace. I don't care how slow you go, just make sure you never come to a complete stop. "Blend" means mix, it means that you are going to have to combine pieces of knowledge along the way to make sense of some things on your path. "Motion" carries great meaning because it asks that you flow, that you travel, that you shift, that you progress; that you identify when you are coming and going, and it asks for understanding and flexibility, just in case you have to journey through some hard times to figure things out.

I am now most interested in what is reflected back to me and I take full responsibility for what I see. Okay, let me back up. Sometimes it takes me a minute. But I get there. As I paint I have become more aware and more curious about what's on the other side of the limit that I am about to push. When I say limit, if you need a visual—think of a ceiling. And when you envision me pushing through that ceiling, you might as well give me a cape.

Turns out this book was about me finding my own strength that was hidden in the shadows.

I lost myself when I lost my brother, and this book reminded me of who I am while reintroducing me to my strength. As you read along, know that I'm reading along right with you, because I like this woman.

I measure my success by the amount of courage I have when I show up for myself and the people I love. I measure it by what is reflected back to me. And any time I do not like the reflection I see, I get curious about what I need to adjust. I do not measure success by my bank account, my job title, by the car that I drive, or the company that I keep. I measure success by the lives I have touched, the hearts I have connected with, and the moments when my energy gives someone permission to see their own worth reflected back at them through my eyes.

In the painting of my life today, I would have to say that I paint with bold, vivid colors.

Painting has allowed me to strengthen every relationship. It enables me to stand in my awareness. I am able to communicate what I need and why I need it. (My husband can't tell the difference between "effective communication" and a "complaint," but that's a whole different book.)

"Parenting" comes with many canvasses! Who knew I would need so many different canvasses just trying to navigate their lives? But I have to say, I'm over here painting masterpieces. I am equipped, untangled, aware, and knowledgeable, and I just helped one of my kids navigate through their first heartbreak. Now, that's living the dream and, in that moment, I felt so alive. It was half past midnight on a school night, and I sat with my child and helped them deal with their pain. And if that's what my success looks and feels like, I will accept that moment over and over again.

"Success" to me is what my children reflect back to me, and it's just that simple. I don't need a million dollars in the bank or ten million followers on social media to feel like I am on top of the world. I feel on top of the world when I help my children work through their feelings. Only in showing up for my own feelings am I able to help them with theirs. Because I paint, I get to teach them how to do the same.

My final canvas for this book is now set up, and I am eager to paint this last scene.

My brother Jared was a tattoo artist in San Francisco. A month or so after his funeral, his tattoo shop held a gathering to celebrate his life and artwork. My sisters and I drove up to be there. We walked around, looking at all of my brother's drawings, hoping for any hidden messages that might make us smile, or just feel better in the moment. I guess when people leave this earth, you just hope you can decode some of the things they left behind. But some of that shit was dark, and we were looking at each other like, "What the hell was he thinking when he drew this?"

The room was full of artists, and two guys approached me and my sister. The artist and his spokesperson, I guess. We were already on the lookout for a sign of hope and we figured this weird approach must be it. When they walked up to us they said something about energy, and a few other things...who knows. We were sad. So we were like, "Alright, we'll entertain this."

We could sense that the two guys before us didn't have an issue with confidence; they appeared armored in that shit.

The spokesperson said, "Art the Artist (this is what we will call him, because I can't remember his name) is going to draw you something without lifting his pen." Seemed interesting, and at that point we were all in. Expectations through the roof.

The artist took out his pen, a 5x5 paper pad, and started. His tool of choice was a Sharpie pen. For sure this guy had to be amazing to use a *permanent marker*, right? I mean, come on, who does that?

The stakes were high, and we were even a little excited.

Art the Artist is all in and about his business. Once finished, he tears the paper from the pad, hands it to us, and walks away.

We were floored. In pure amazement. Speechless. When we turned that paper over, what appeared before us blew our minds.

The drawing looked as if we had handed a two-year-old a crayon to keep them busy.

I guess my brother had laughter bottled up for us—because we have never laughed so hard in the midst of pain. But that's not why I'm telling this story.

> ***I'm telling this story because the artist had enough sense to believe in himself. Enough belief to create what he could attach meaning to.***

Whether I believed in him or not didn't make a bit of difference to him. He was already armored in confidence and when you're armored in confidence you can be and do whatever you want. He believed in himself. In his approach, he had already arrived. He was not waiting for anyone to validate what he already saw in himself.

My sister and I laughed for the rest of the night because we kept telling each other the story over and over again while laying together on a queen-sized bed, in a hotel room three hundred and sixty-two miles away from home. Our other two sisters wished we would just go to sleep. But we were too busy reliving a moment that we would remember, and in a weird way cherish, forever.

As I applied the last color to this canvas for flow purposes, I decided that I am not going to drop or throw the paintbrushes, nor am I going to lay them down. I'm not even going to take the time to rinse them off. I'm just going to give them to you.

Life will provide the canvases you need, your courage is the paint, and I just provided your tools.

NOW IT'S UP TO YOU TO PAINT.

ABOUT THE AUTHOR

....

Sicola Elliott penned her first book, "Pocket Book of Poems from a Teenage Heart," at a young age, and is the creator of the "My Teenage Heart Collection" motivational cards. While successfully operating her own childcare business, Ms. Elliott decided to switch gears and follow her heart's calling—motivating teenage girls and women to live their lives with vibrant, colorful intention. Through speaking and facilitating workshops, Ms. Elliott has captivated and motivated the hearts and minds of thousands. Her love for words and desire to illuminate the personal growth process for others prompted Ms. Elliott to lay bare her own transformational process and bring a fresh voice to the world of personal development through this book. Ms. Elliott is currently pursuing a B.A. in Community Psychology from Pacific Oaks College and resides in Long Beach, California with her husband and three children.

JARED,

THiS MASTERPieCe

is FOR YOU. ♡

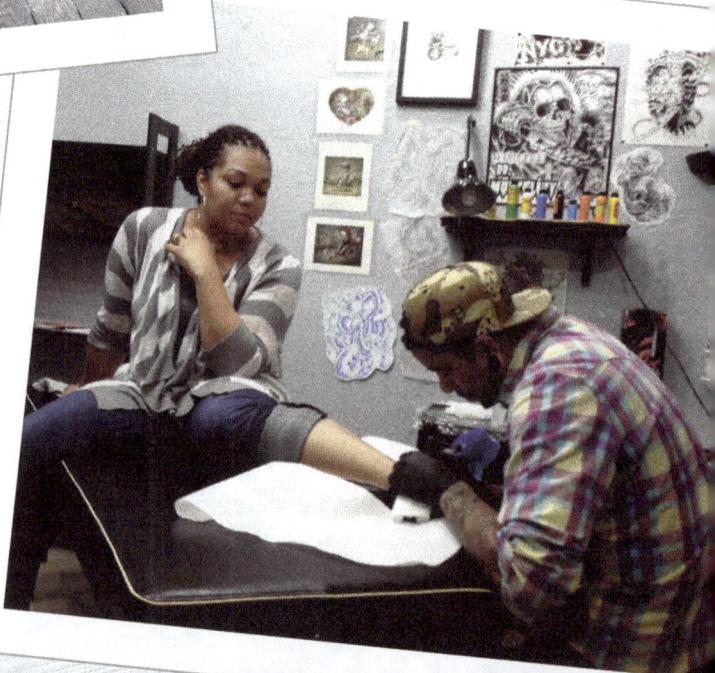

www.ingramcontent.com/pod-product-compliance
Lightning Source LLC
Chambersburg PA
CBHW071844090426
42811CB00035B/2321/J